CONTENTS

ACKNOWLEDGMENTS

Portions of the activity section of this guide represent the work of the following Goleta Union School District Personnel, which appeared in the "Perceptual Development Guide" published in 1968.

Mildred Farnum, Goleta Union School District

Sara Gelb, Saint Vincent's School, Santa Barbara

Dennis Naiman, Goleta Union School District

Jean Vroman, Goleta Union School District

John Kuizenga, Goleta Union School District

Special gratitutde is due to A. Jean Ayres, PhD, for the knowledge and challenge she has presented.

Thanks to Pat Wilbarger for her assistance in interpreting sensorimotor theory. Without her assistance this guide would not be possible.

Appreciation is owed to the following persons who have also been instrumental in the development of this guide:

G. William Elliott, PhD, Director ESEA Title III Perceptual-Motor Development Project

Linda Faria, OTR, Perceptual-Motor Specialist

Marian Anderson, Professor Emeritus, University of California, Santa Barbara

Sara Gelb, Consultant, Saint Vincent's School, Santa Barbara

Jeannette Lenger, Primary Teacher, Orcutt Unified School District

Bud Robinson, Guidance Specialist, Goleta Union School District

The developers are indebted to Lee Neill, Miller-Unruh Guidance Specialist, for her helpful criticism and assistance.

Appreciation is due to Maria Kakis for her special consultation and assistance.

This book originated as an ESEA Title III Project, Number 5127, "Identification, Diagnosis and Remediation of Sensorimotor Dysfunction in Primary School Children." Subsequently, it became a publication of the Goleta, California, School District, which appeared in two volumes produced by the Santa Barbara County Super Intendent of Schools' Office.

FOREWORD

This publication is the outgrowth of a need among Title III project participants to implement sensorimotor theory into effective remedial activities for use in public schools. The publication should be considered a working manual for project participants.

Terminology used in this manual presumes the reader's basic understanding of sensorimotor theory and its implementation.

The primary theoretical structure to which this project subscribes is that of Dr. A. Jean Ayres.

This manual is by no means an exhaustive attempt to locate or devise sensorimotor remedial activities. It is, rather, an attempt to supply the primary classroom teacher with specimen activities within the Ayres theoretical framework on which to expand.

The remedial activities contained within this guide represent the efforts of (1) Dr. A. Jean Ayres, (2) other authors of perceptual-motor theory as listed in the bibliography, and (3) experts in elementary school physical education.

This program is centered around the treatment of causes of sensorimotor dysfunction rather than the effects, which we believe makes this program distinctive from other attempts at the remediation of perceptual-motor deficits.

STRUCTURE OF THE GUIDE AS BASED ON SYNDROMES OF SENSORIMOTOR DYSFUNCTION

Postural and Bilateral Motor Integration

    A.   Primitive postural responses (tonic neck reflex and tonic labyrinthine reflex)
    B.   Equilibrium reaction
    C.   Integration of the two body sides
    D.   Left-right discrimination
    E.   Visual perception of a horizontal sequence in space

Apraxia

    A.   Tactile function
        1.   "protective" system
        2.   "discriminative" system
    B.   Kinesthetic function
    C.   Gross-motor planning
    D.   Fine-motor planning, eye-hand coordination

Form and Space Perception

    A.   Space perception
    B.   Form perception
    C.   Figure ground

Tactile Defensiveness or Disinhibition

Disorder of the Left Body Side

Cognitive Skills

DEFINED SENSORIMOTOR CATEGORIES

The theoretical structure of the activity guide is adapted from the work of A. Jean Ayres, PhD. The syndromes of sensorimotor dysfunction discussed in the following pages are considered distinct but interrelated areas of function.

POSTURAL AND BILATERAL MOTOR INTEGRATION

A. Primitive postural responses

The tonic neck reflex and tonic labyrinthine reflex are involuntary but essential responses to stimuli that occur in infancy. For example, when an infant of three months turns his head, one may see extensor tone in the extremities the child is facing and flexor tone in the opposing extremities. At approximately the same age, the predominant muscle tone in the infant is flexion in the prone position. In the supine position, extensor tone predominates. These reflexes are important phases of the child's development and are entirely normal. Usually these reflexes gradually diminish (are inhibited) and the higher levels of righting and equilibrium reactions take their place. If these reflexes are not properly inhibited, an individual may have inadequate muscle tone, posture, balance, and coordination.

Sample activities:

Tonic Neck Reflex—Inhibition involves positioning in remedial activity with the arm on the face side flexed and the arm on the skull side extended, usually while the child is in a quadrupedal position. A sheet entitled "Positions for Inhibition of the TNR" has been prepared and is available through A. Jean Ayres, PhD.

Tonic Labyrinthine Reflex—Inhibition for remediation should involve positioning in an arched back posture (extension) when prone, and in a knees-to-chest or in a totally flexed posture when supine. Prone on a scooter board, the child rides down an incline board into a stack of cardboard boxes.

B. Equilibrium reaction

This is the righting reflex, an antigravity response. The previously mentioned postural reflexes (tonic neck and tonic labyrinthine) should be inhibited prior to *focusing* in this area. This is not to say equilibrium activities cannot be performed concurrently with tonic neck reflex and tonic labyrinthine reflex activities.

It is presumed that, if the child has to think consciously about balance (or use a higher cortical level), he will have a more difficult time focusing on more important academic activities. Postural responses should be encouraged to occur at the subcortical (midbrain) level. If you try too hard to elicit an equilibrium reaction, it will be at the cortical level and not an automatic response.

The first responses opposing gravity are in the prone position, then quadrupedal and bipedal, so the remedial activities should advance in similar fashion. At the bipedal level of equilibrium reaction, activities should involve trunk rotation.

When the child is able to integrate the two hemispheres of the brain, he may be ready to progress to activities using the two body sides in an integrated manner.

Sample activity:

The child lies prone on a large ball, meanwhile holding the teacher's wrist. The child moves himself about on the ball to elicit equilibrium reactions.

C. Integration of the two body sides

Following inhibition of the primitive postural reflexes and maturation of the equilibrium function (which provides the foundation), subsequent steps may be taken, the next of which is integration of the two body sides.

Integration of the two body sides includes first and most importantly use of the two body sides together (bilaterality), and secondly, activities that contrast body sides (reciprocal movement such as flexion with one arm and extension with the other simultaneously).

Children who have trouble integrating the two body sides may also experience difficulty crossing the body midline.

Sample activities:

> *Emphasizing body sides* (bilaterality)—The child is positioned with legs astride on an automobile tire, jumping bilaterality in circles.

> *Contrasting body sides* (reciprocal)—The child is lying prone on a scooter, and propels the body through an obstacle course, alternating hands.

D. Left-right discrimination

This develops out of an awareness of body sides (laterality). The kindergarten child may not be aware of the coinciding names for body sides (directionality).

To perceive left and right outside the body is more sophisticated, and involves position-in-space and spatial relations.

Sample activity:

Crawling unilaterally while straddling a painted line, may help the child become more aware of sidedness.

Directionality is knowing the coordinates of space (left, right, up, down, and finally behind and in front).

E. Visual perception of a horizontal sequence in space

Directional treatment in this area should begin with inhibition of primitive postural reflexes, equilibrium reactions, etc., but may also occur at a more advanced stage, i.e., a reversal problem such as confusing *was* for *saw*, *d* for *b*, etc.

Sample activity:

Horizontal sequencing in space, grossly oversimplified, is the ability to place blocks, beads, letters in a horizontal sequence as they appear on a pattern. Reading is also a form of horizontal sequencing.

APRAXIA

Apraxia is the reduced capacity to perform planned movement, due in part to a disorder of sensory integration.

A. Tactile function
It is thought the tactile function is normalized by attempting (1) to

balance the *protective system* (the primitive system designed primarily to warn off impending danger) and (2) educate the *discrimitive tactile system* (the system which conveys information about the environment to the child). Enhancement of the discriminating tactile system is obtained partly through inhibition of a protective response. Remediation involves stimulation of pressure receptors by encouraging body contact with pressure. Tactile activities should be on or below the child's ability to motor plan.

Sample activity:

Log rolling on carpet and holding an eraser between the knees, the child goes to and from a specific point.

B. Kinesthetic function

Kinesthesis is a feeling within the body for extent, direction or weight of movement. The sensing organs for kinesthesia are located in the muscles, tendons, and joints which receive a continuous supply of information about movement. Unlike the tactile function, which is information obtained by the skin from external stimuli, the kinesthetic impressions come from internal stimuli. It is the combination of tactile and kinesthetic experiences which develop body schema (knowledge of body parts, their relationship to one another, and the ability to visualize them in movement). As body schema is enhanced through sensory integration of the tactile and kinesthetic system, so is the ability to motor plan.

Sample activity:

Lying prone on a scooter board riding down an incline board, the child brakes himself by catching a long strip of inner tube (6 inches by 3 inches) held one foot off the floor by persons at either end.

C. Gross motor planning

Gross motor planning is the ability to perform planned movement in an integrated and coordinated fashion. As sensory perception matures (including the tactile and kinesthetic function), so also does the child's ability to execute a planned movement. Early in life the child must plan out movements such as rolling, crawling, and sitting. As proficiency is gained, these responses are no longer planned motor acts, but rather become automatic responses.

For those exhibiting difficulty with planned gross movement, motor planning activities are to be preceded by, or administered concurrently with, tactile and kinesthetic activities. Should you be working on the child's level developmentally, and should the child be still experiencing difficulty, take him passively through the activity. The feedback received from the kinesthetic system will assist him in developing body scheme. Activities should utilize basic postures (arched back position, quadrupedal, sitting, etc.) and the whole body first, prior to performing activities involving the body extremities.

Sample activity:

The child moves an obstacle course incorporating such basic motor planning activities as crawling, creeping, rolling, etc.

D. Fine motor planning. Eye-hand coordination

This involves the ability to perform planned movement of the fine muscle groups, i.e., hands, fingers, etc.

Activities listed in this section are developmentally more sophisticated than those listed under Gross Motor Planning.

Sample activity:

Cut, from cardboard, geometric figures outlined with heavy black lines.

SPACE AND FORM PERCEPTION

A. Space perception

During infancy a child perceives the distance and direction of objects in relationship to the position of his own body (position-in-space). From this primitive ability he learns to perceive the position of one object in relation to another, that is, is spatial relationships.

If space perception is poor, there may be a dysfunction in the vestibular system. It is through the vestibular system that one knows which way the head is in relation to the horizon.

Sample activity:

The manipulation of large blocks (cardboard or wood) gives the child experience making spatial judgments involving the entire body, as does experience moving through exact space, e.g., walking between the wall and an object held vertically, close enough to the wall that the child must turn sideways to pass between the wall and the object.

The previously mentioned activities could be labeled "gross space perception." Finer forms of space perception include: *Frostig Work*

Sheets: Position in Space, Spatial Relations, and Form Constancy.

B. Form perception

Prime factors in the development of form perception are: (1) the ability of the eyes to follow along and receive kinesthetic feedback from the eye muscles to the brain, and (2) kinesthetic feedback from other body parts: mouth, fingers, etc.

1. Shape:

Where constancy of shape is concerned, two- and three-dimensional forms are recognized as belonging to certain categories of shapes, whatever their size, color, texture, mode of representation, or angle seen by the perceiver.

2. Size:

This is the ability to perceive the actual size of an object, regardless of factors that may change its apparent size.

Sample activity:

Line up balls or blocks of various sizes at varying distances and have the child point out or pick out the largest or smallest items, regardless of their distance from him.

3. Color:

This is the ability to recognize colors, regardless of background or conditions of illumination. (A red book is recognized as that, regardless of the illumination in the room.)

Sample activity:

Can the child recognize white as such even though the illumination varies from dim to very bright?

The highest level of form perception is matching, which is included under Cognitive Skills.

C. Figure ground

This is the ability of an observer to select and attend to one set of stimuli, while keeping the majority in the dimly perceived ground.

A child bouncing a ball on the playground has her attention directed to the ball, which is the figure in the scene she perceives. Since other features of the playground (sandbox, teeter-totter, flower bed, toy pail) are not the focus of her attention; they form the dimly perceived ground, of which she is probably only sufficiently aware to avoid collision.

Sample activity:

Gross activities include hitting a moving target. Fine activities include the ability to distinguish the figure from the ground on worksheets involving colors, sizes, textures, dimensions, and outlining.

TACTILE DEFENSIVENESS

Tactile defensiveness is characterized by an aversive or defensive reaction to tactile and other stimulation. Reactions may be: to flee, fight, display emotionally unstable characteristics, make excuses to avoid tactile encounters. Children with these observed reactions may be restless, distractable, and often oversensitive to sound. See Apraxia.

In addition to tactile and auditory defensiveness, olfactory defensiveness make up the three most fundamental sensory channels which warn if danger is present.

Of the two tactile subsystems (protective and discriminative), inhibition of the protective tactile response is that which is most closely linked with tactile defensiveness.

Submerging the protective system will help eliminate tactile defensiveness and make the discriminative system more responsive.

Tactually defensive children may prefer remedial measures which involve individual patterns of sensory stimulation and often include touch pressure and slow vestibular stimulation and occasionally light touch.

It is strongly recommended that any form of tactile stimulation should not be imposed upon the child against his wishes but rather follow his own inclination for tactile stimuli.

Sample activity:

Lying on a carpet, the child imagines he has just come out of the ocean, and must dry his entire body by bringing it into contact with the carpet. Pretend the carpet is a beach towel.

DISORDERS OF THE LEFT BODY SIDE

Disorders of the left body side are characterized by more difficulty with function on the left body side as in contrast to the right body side. It is *thought* that left-side disorders *may be* due to dysfunction of the right cerebral hemisphere—which, incidentally, is not identical to the left cerebral hemisphere.

Remedial activities include inhibition of primitive postural reflexes and integration of the two body sides. Another possible source of remediation may be equilibrium responses.

COGNITIVE SKILLS RELATED TO VISUAL CONCEPTUALIZATION

Visual Conceptualization: Conceptualizing what we see.

1. Recognition: Accurate interpretation.

Sample activity:

The child learns to recognize a square as such.

2. Discrimination: To differentiate between.

Sample activity:

The child learns to distinguish one letter from another.

3. Matching: Ability to see similarities.

Sample activity:

Matching buttons of the same color, shape, and size.

4. Memory:

  a. motor—ability to recall movements of the component parts of a motor activity.

  b. visual—ability to recall the image of a form, letter or word.

  c. auditory—amount of information an individual can retain in proper sequence, particularly for purposes of immediate action or recall.

5. Use in abstract:

Sample activity:

The child gains the ability to describe the back side of an object, although only the front is visible.

CHARACTERISTICS SOMETIMES EXHIBITED

DEFICIT IN POSTURAL AND BILATERAL INTEGRATION

1. A tendency for other parts of the body (arms, shoulders, torso) to move simultaneously as head moves.
2. A lack of integrated coordination of the two body sides.
3. Difficulty maintaining the arched back posture (pivot prone position) due to residual flexor tone; will try to avoid the arched back posture.
4. Poor equilibrium reactions standing and hopping.
5. Head held forward.
6. Ability to perform rhythmic movement and to reproduce rhythmic sequence below par for age.
7. Poor muscle tone (tense or flaccid).
8. One extremity not as active as the other.
9. Stance sometimes unequal, the weight being on the stronger or dominant side of the body.
10. A lack of ability to make an adaptive response on the large plastic ball.
11. Difficulty jumping with both feet (bilateral coordination).
12. Difficulty clapping out a rhythm with both hands.
13. Avoidance of crossing the body midline during general activities.
14. Difficulty crossing the midline with the eyes.
15. Difficulty distinguishing body sides (kindergarten children are often not aware of the concept of left and right).
16. Inability to balance, and subsequent trouble with spatial relations.
17. Difficulty perceiving the vertical, often hinders balance.
18. Endomorphs (robust body type) are more likely to have difficulty in the bilateral posture motor integration syndrome.

APRAXIA

1. Excessive clumsiness when approaching new tasks.
2. Reduced capacity to perform planned movement.
3. Lack of kinesthetic awareness (feeling within the body for what it is doing).

4. Uneven and hesitant gait.
5. Inability to locate the exact point of stimulation (knowing where he was touched).
6. Difficulty identifying the fingers as they are touched.
7. Messy handwriting.
8. Difficulty tracing over another line.
9. Poor tactile perception.
10. Difficulty imitating body postures.
11. Poor ocular control.
12. Lack of body awareness.
13. Inclined toward emotional instability.
14. Ectomorphs (slight body build) more likely to be apraxic.

DEFICIT IN SPACE AND FORM PERCEPTION

1. Inability to put puzzles together which offer no difficulty to peers.
2. Inability to recognize letters and numbers.
3. Inability to draw basic geometric shapes and match them to each other visually.
4. Inability to differentiate background from foreground in a picture.
5. Inability to relate objects to each other with regard to spatial relationships; unable to block-build with some order.
6. Inability to demonstrate the ability to relate the body to environmental space; unable to move between or through objects guided by vision and an awareness of body dimensions.
7. Difficulty balancing. It is through the vestibular system (balance) that one learns which way the head is in relation to the earth.

TACTILE DEFENSIVENESS

1. Negative response to being touched.
2. Craving to be touched.
3. Hyperactivity frequently present.
4. Hypermobility frequently present.
5. Hypersensitivity to high-frequency sound, bright lights, odors.
6. Difficulty in concentrating.
7. Significant response on a tactile test.

8. Tendency to fight when standing in line or in crowds.

9. Tendency to spend time with adults and children whose movement patterns are more predictable.

10. Tendency to avoid contact on the body extremities by wearing a coat, even though it may not be necessary. Clothes which irritate the skin (tweed, etc.) may be avoided in favor of nonirritating materials such as silk, nylon, etc.

11. Hypersensitivity to hair combing or face washing.

INABILITY TO USE THE LEFT BODY SIDE (OR RIGHT CEREBRAL HEMISPHERE)

1. Avoidance of using the left body side.

2. Decreased muscle tone on one body side.

3. Lowering of the shoulder on one side.

4. Avoidance of holding a paper with the left hand while coloring with the right.

5. Difference on the right and left scores in perceptual testing.

6. Frequent difficulty turning to the left coming down on an incline board.

7. Difficulty doing tonic neck reflex exercises on the left side of the body.

HINTS

Activity programs are thought to be more effective if:

The activities follow the developmental sequence for each syndrome.

Activities whenever possible should demand an adaptive response from the child.

Each activity has a definite beginning and end.

Be purposeful in that each activity has interest and meaning for the individual. The child should be emotionally involved in the activity. Use exercises only as a last resort.

Begin from simple and progress toward complex patterns.

Emphasize gross movement first and progress to fine movement.

Each member of the group should work on or below his own developmental level as much as possible.

Repetition is valuable if motivation is not sacrificed.

Remediations of perceptual deficits are thought to be more effective at the primary level.

Remedial activities are performed more than once daily in short periods (15-30 mins.) as the child's attention span and interest permit.

RECOMMENDED EQUIPMENT

The following equipment is recommended on the basis of its relationship to Dr. Ayres' theory and its versatility. Of primary concern are those pieces of equipment to implement the Ayres theory (e.g., scooter board, Spastickerballe, etc.). Next in priority, equipment with which numerous activities (within the Ayres framework) may be performed. These pieces of equipment are listed under Group A. It is recommended that equipment listed under Group A be purchased prior to equipment listed under B and C, which are more limited in their use.

Those items preceded by an asterisk should be purchased in sufficient numbers so there is one item for every five children. On items with a double asterisk, one unit per child would be ideal.

NAMES AND ADDRESSES OF COMPANIES WHO STOCK RECOMMENDED GROSS MOTOR EQUIPMENT

Blende's Mission Music Co.
106 West Mission Street
Santa Barbara, California

Bowmar Records, Inc.
10515 Burbank Boulevard, North
Hollywood, California 91601

Childcraft Equipment Co., Inc.
155 East 23rd Street
New York, New York 10010

Creative Playthings, Inc.
5757 West Century Boulevard
Los Angeles, California 90045

Custom Fidelity Records
Hidden Valley Hideout
133 San Miguel Road
Pasadena, California

Developmental Design
    P.O. Box 55
    Carpinteria, California 93013

Educational Activities, Inc.
    P.O. Box 392
    Freeport, New York

Educational Record Sales
    157 Chambers Street
    New York, New York 10007

Hanover House
    Hanover, Pennsylvania 17331

Health Institute of America
    c/o Fountain Head
    4314 East Indian School Road
    Phoenix, Arizona 85018

James H. Heineman, Inc.
    60 East 42nd Street
    New York, New York

Le Crone Rhythm Records, Inc.
    9203 Nichols Road
    Oklahoma City, Oklahoma 73120

Lyndoncraft
    P.O. Box 12
    Rosemead, California 91770

Oregon Worsted Company
    8300 South East McLoughlin Boulevard
    Portland, Oregon

Physical Education Supply Asso., Inc.
    P.O. Box 292
    Trumbull, Connecticut 06611

J. A. Preston Corp.
    71 Fifth Avenue
    New York, New York 10003

Program Aids Company, Inc.
    No. 1, Physical Fitness Drive
    Garden, New York 11530

Rhythms Record Company
9203 Nichols Road
Oklahoma City, Oklahoma 73120

Sears, Roebuck & Co.
Los Angeles, California 90054

Sporthaus Maul
6 Frankfurt am Main
Neve Mainzer
Strabe West Germany

W. J. Voit Rubber Corp.
3801 South Harbor Boulevard
Santa Ana, California 92704

Wolverine Sports
745 State Circle
Ann Arbor, Michigan

Young People Records—Childrens Record Guild
100 Sixth Avenue
New York, New York

RECOMMENDED GROSS MOTOR EQUIPMENT
(Prices shown are approximate)

GROUP A

Scooter Boards—Developmental Design, O2A, $14.50, four-wheeled scooter "designed to assist children's progress through early developmental stages."

Spastickerballe—Sporthaus Maul, medium size 29" -30", $12.50; small size 23" -24", $10.00.

**Rope*—Any hardware or marine supply store, 3/8" polypropylene or nylon No. 10 sash cord. K-3 indiv. rope 7' -8'. Long rope 15' -18'. Per foot, $.09 to $.12; usually discounted in large quantities.

**Hula Hoops*—Sears, Roebuck and Co., ½" flexible plastic pipe, $5.48/100', ¾", $4.79/50', plastic connections, $.19 each, 8½' length makes a hoop slightly less than 3' in diameter.

Inner Tubes—Service stations (usually free) both truck and car tubes. Tubes which are not repairable can be cut into strips and bands for kinesthetic activities.

Bounce Boards—Lyndoncraft, 405A, $24.50.

Cardboard Boxes—Small boxes (to hit coming off an incline on a scooter board, to climb in and out of, for use as markers or obstacles). Large TV or refrigerator boxes, cut holes of various sizes and shapes (triangles, rectangles, etc.) from the box side and top for climbing in and out of.

*Barrels (cardboard)—Health food stores, schools (sweeping compound); sometimes free, usually a minimal charge.

*Mats—Wolverine Sports, foam-filled vinyl covered, 2" x 2' x 6', $27.95; nylon strip fasteners hold them together. Program Aids, Co., Inc., Lite-Weight Mats with Wonder-Lite Core, 2" x 4 x 6'. Zippers for snug end-to-end hitching; No. M54, $45.00.

*Foam Strips—Upholstery shop or wholesale foam outlet, 3' x 6' x approximately $7.00.

*Weighted wrist, ankle, and waist belts—Wolverine Sports, adjustable ankle weight bands, DE-25, 2-½ lbs. apiece, $7.95 pair; adjustable wrist bands, No. ST-25, 2-½lbs. apiece, $6.95 a pair (for kinesthetic awareness activities).

Large Cardboard Blocks—Creative Playthings, Play-Core hollow corrugated cardboard blocks. Half-School Set: 16 unit blocks, 16 double units, 8 quadruple units, DP-501, $19.75 (for spatial awareness activities).

Incline Board—Wolverine Sports, high school high-jump standards, $19.95 a pair. Place a ¾" x 4' x 8' sheet of plywood on the adjustable brackets (underside of the plywood sheet should be rigged so the plywood does not slip off the high-jump standard brackets). A gradually sloping natural incline is also suitable.

Platform Swing—Developmental Design, 03A, $19.95, 2-½' square of ½" plywood with a fiberglass surface for added strength and grip. Includes ropes and special yoke which gives this swing its unstable qualities (for equilibrium responses, kinesthetic input, and motor planning activities).

**Terry Cloth Towel (bath size)

Hammock—Hanover House, $6.98 + $.85 postage on a single order. Pocket-size green hammocks to suspend and swing or spin child in.

Exercise Wheel—Health Institute of America, single rubber wheel with handles on both sides. A variety of co-contraction activities are the wheels primary value. Junior Model, $4.99.

GROUP B

Beach Ball—Most toy stores or discount houses, circumference 28", constructed of thin gauge plastic.

Tumble Tub—Creative Playthings, CP100E, $14.95.

*Scoops and Ball—Scoops are cut from plastic bleach bottles. Any rubber ball or the "whiffle" ball is adequate.

*Streamers—Crepe paper or plastic streamers on a short piece of dowling.

Balance Boards—Developmental Design, 01A, $14.50; 2' square of ¾" plywood with a specially constructed dome base.

T-Stools—Developmental Design, one-legged stool, 04A, $7.50 (equilibrium response).

Punch Balls—J.C. Penney & Co., $.39 (basic catching activities).

Mirror—Western Auto Supply, full-length nonbreakable mirror, approximately $5.00; or any glass company.

Fleece Balls—Oregon Worsted Co., No. 3, $10.68/dozen.

Records:

Type of Record

Relaxation—Educational Activities Inc., *Relaxation-Impulse Control Through Relaxation,* AR 655 1-12" 33-1/3 record "To aid hyperactive and over-aroused children to reduce their levels of activation."

Creative Movement—Le Crone Rhythm Records, Inc., *Creative Rhythms,* RRC 2103. A variety of times, tempos, moods, and styles to encourage creative expression of movement presented on piano and organ.

Creative Movement—Le Crone Rhythm Records, Inc., *Creative*

Rhythms, RRC 103. Action and innovative rhythms, 24 separate rhythms, piano and voice.

Basic Rhythms—Bowman Records, Inc., *Rhythm Time* (walk, run), (short rope and long rope), mirror image (a leader initiates the movement, children follow), ball handling. B 2058 LP.

Rope Jumping and Ball Handling Rhythms—Bowmar Records, Inc., *Rope Jumping and Ball Handling,* rope jumping rhythms (short rope and long rope). Mirror image (a leader initiates the movement, children follow). Ball handling. B 2058 LP.

Creative Rhythms— James H. Heineman, Inc., *Come Dance With Me,* Free Movement Rhythmic Dance Book and record (water, the clock, the bouncing ball, the storm).

Creative Movement—RCA, *Little Duck,* LE 101. A little duck swims out to sea and is rescued by a sea gull.
Ballons, LE 104. For free expression and simple technique.
Flappy and Floppy, LE 106. The lighthearted rag-doll puppet whose strings break.
Magic Mountain, LE 103. A land of fantasy and enchantment.
Noah's Ark, LE 102. And all the animals who came two by two.
The Toy Tree, LE 107. Come and see what is growing on the toy tree.

Body Awareness—Educational Activities Inc., *Listening and Moving,* LP 605. The development of body awareness and position in space.

Creative Movement—Young People Records, *My Playful Scarf,* 1-10'', 78 RPM, CRG 1019, $1.24. Designed to give children an opportunity for rhythmic expression with a minimum of supervision.

Creative Movement—Young People Records, *Train to the Zoo,* 1-10'', 78 RPM, CRG 1001, $1.24. Children can carry out activities of those zoo animals suggested by song.

Rhythmic Patterning—Young People Records, *Nothing to Do,* 1-10'', 78 RPM, CRG 1012, $1.24. Includes rhythmic patterns for marching, tip-toeing, spinning, clapping hands and other expressions.

Creative Movement—Young People Records, *Little Puppet,* 1-10'', 78 RPM, CRG 1016, $1.24. Child imitates puppet gestures to rhythmic music of French folk songs. Lyrics suggest what he is to do.

Creative Movement—Educational Record Sales, *Rhythms for Today,* 2-12″, 33-1/3 RPM, $10.95. Children are helped to respond rhythmically through the use of familiar sounds: clock ticks, monkey chatter, witches' screech, drumming, clang of fire engines, rockets blasting off, etc.

Creative Movement—Educational Record Sales, *Rhythmic Activities, Volume 1,* 1-12″, 33-1/3 RPM, $6.25. Produced by Florence Bassett and Cora Mae Chestnut. The accompaniments on these records are for simple rhythmic activities such as running, skipping, jumping, bouncing, swinging.

Creative Movement—Educational Record Sales, *Happy Times,* 1-12″, 33-1/3 RPM, K-1, $4.95. Sixteen singing games involving partner choosing, acting out stories of familiar tasks, and free creative action.

Creative Movement— Educational Record Sales, *Classroom Rhythms, Rhythms of Cowboys and Indians,* 1-12″, 33-1/3 RPM, K-2, $5.95. Children are helped to feel, hear, then move rhythmically.

Creative Movement and Patterned Movement—Educational Record Sales, *Developing Body Articulation,* 1-12″, 33-1/3 RPM, $5.95. The songs of this record require the child's active participation. Through specific activities associated with each song, he progresses from global movements, positions and related body concepts to finely differentiated and discrete conceptual-motor patterns and units.

Directionality—Rhythm Record Company, *For Primary Readiness and Number Readiness,* RRC 203. In, out, left, right, up, down.

Directionality—Custom Fidelity Records, *Suzita Says Together We Learn,* CF 1299. To differentiate left from right is the focus.

Rhythm Sticks (Claves)—Childcraft, 9″ hardwood sticks, $1.50 a pair.

Rubber Rings—Physical Education Supply Associated, Inc. Tennis rings, $1.65, Approximately 6″ diameter.

Balls—W. J. Voit Rubber Co. Utility balls—Voit recommended
No. 6—$1.35
No. 7—$1.65

No. 8-½—$2.25
No. 10—$2.35
No. 13—$2.95
No. 16—$3.95
Kickball (deluxe) Utility No. 8, yellow only, CG8—$3.55.

Trim Twist—The executive exerciser. Develops rotation of the trunk which may assist the righting reflex. Approximately $5.95 at leading department stores.

Twister Game—Milton Bradley, good for planned movement as directed.

Equilibrium Swing—Developmental Design, $11.50. Circular disc cut from the finest grade of ¾" plywood with a suspending rope. An expansion spring is spliced into the rope above the child's grasp, which gives the child vestibular (balance) stimulation in the up and down plane, as well as forward, backward and laterally. Child sits on the disc bouncing, and swinging.

GROUP C

Rubber Hands and Feet—Creative Playthings, A J06 Feet, $4.50; A J02 Hands, $4.50.

Tunnel—Childcraft, Tunnel of Fun, 7A 182, $9.95. Fabric covering a spring steel frame. Easily collapsible.

Stairs—Childcraft, Walk a Plank, $39.00. Pair of stairs, with a beam (2" x 4"). The beam may be placed between the separated stairs thus, walk the plank.

Medicine Ball—Physical Education Supply Associated, Inc. Inflated type: 11-½", $7.25, 4.4 lbs.; 7-¾", $4.75, 2.2 lbs. (for lifting and accompanying proprioceptive input).

Cardboard Sled—Heavy cardboard with rope handle, 2½' x 4' (equilibrium reactions).

Tether Ball—Physical Education Associated Supply, Inc., RA 599, $3.00.

Colored Tapes—Wolverine Sport, red, green, blue, black, yellow: 36 yards ½", $1.39; 60 yards 1", $3.49; 60 yards 2", $5.25.

Game Cones—Wolverine Sports, Olympia Game Cones, 18" bright orange, $3.99 each.

Plastic Tubes—Educational Activities, Inc., Pla-tubes, twelve 36''
hollow tubes, $5.25.

Olympia Rings—Novo Educational Toy and Equipment Corp., 2 ½''
Olympia hoops, 10'' diameter (approximate). Four 19'' Olympia sticks. With a stick in each hand two children play catch
with the hoops. No. 11026 $2.20.

Key-Wound Metronome—Novo Educational Toy and Equipment
Corp., beat and tempo from 40 to 208 beats per minute. Size,
9'' x 4½''. In durable birch case, mahogany or walnut finish.
No. 50 B, $14.95.

Quoit Set—Novo Educational Toy and Equipment Co., two 7-½''
round wood bases with four colored Flexo-Quoits, 6'' diameter.
A hand-eye coordination, spatial perception and bilateral
activity. Child holds a single wood base in both hands and rings
the quoits thrown to him. No. 8073, $4.75.

*Plumber's Friend—Hardware store or plumbing supply (paddle
for scooter board activities).

SUGGESTED MATERIALS
IN OTHER SPECIFIC AREAS

Eye-Hand Coordination, Fine Motor Planning, Form Perception, Form Constancy, Tactile Discrimination, Body Awareness, Figure Ground, Space Perception, and Visual Conceptualization.

The perceptual materials listed in the following pages are specimens
categorized in the perceptual areas mentioned above.

There are numerous materials available to supplement those listed.
Additional materials should be selected as they relate to the specific
objectives of remediation.

The materials were divided into areas they seem *most related* to,
with the knowledge they almost always overlap into other areas.
These other areas are sometimes listed in parentheses should use of
the material be particularly important to remediation in another area.

Information following the material trade name is in most cases that
of the manufacturer. It should be pointed out that use of these materials will not in most cases by themselves remediate for dysfunction
in the area under which they are listed.

NAMES AND ADDRESSES
OF COMPANIES WHO STOCK
RECOMMENDED MATERIALS

American Seating
945 West Hyde Park Boulevard
Inglewood, California 90302

Art Chemical Co.
Huntington, Indiana

California Association for Neurologically
Handicapped Children, San Francisco Chapter
P.O. Box 16380
San Francisco, California 94116

Childcraft Equipment Co., Inc.
155 East 23rd Street
New York, New York 10010

Continental Press
2085 East Foothill
Pasadena, California

Developmental Learning Materials (DLM)
3505 North Ashland Avenue
Chicago, Illinois 60657

Lakeshore Equipment Company (Lakeshore)
P.O. Box 2116
1144 Montague Avenue
San Leandro, California 94577

Noble and Noble Publishers, Inc.
750 Third Avenue
New York, New York 10017

Novo Educational Toy and Equipment Co.
585 Avenue of the Americas (Sixth Avenue)
New York, New York 10011

Teaching Aids by Laurl Enterprises
Phillips-Avon, Maine 04966

Teaching Resources
100 Boylston Street
Boston, Massachusetts 02116

The Frostig Program for the Development
of Visual Perception, Follett Publishing Co.
1010 West Washington Boulevard
Chicago, Illinois

The Instructor Publications, Inc.
Dansville, New York 14437

Tri-Counties Educational Materials Center
4020 Calle Real
Santa Barbara, California 93105

Winter Haven Lions Research Foundation, Inc.
P.O. Box 1045
Winter Haven, Florida 33880

SUGGESTED PERCEPTUAL MATERIALS
(Prices shown are approximate)

FORM PERCEPTION, FORM CONSTANCY

Winter Haven Materials—Teacher Perceptual Testing and Training
Kits for first grade, total kit $14.00. For kindergarten, total
kit $16.00. Winter Haven Lions Research Foundation.

Fit A Space—Sixteen crepe foam rubber form boards in four colors
to be fitted with 49 cut-out rubber inserts. Children are end-
lessly fascinated with these small puzzles that may be matched
by color and shape or fitted in contrasting colors. Catalog No.
LR68, $3.25, Lakeshore.

Fit A Shape—24 crepe foam rubber graduated shapes to fit in matching panels. Shapes in contrasting colors. Designed for preschool
children to learn common shapes in relative sizes. Catalog No.
LR80, $3.25, Lakeshore.

Experiences for Young Children, Tasks 1, 2, and 3—Task 1: An
exercise in discriminating basic geometric shapes first by shape,
then by size, then by rotation. Task 2: The child encounters
more intricate design patterns created with three dimensional
red and white blocks. Task 3: He uses alphabet tiles to create
words and word groups as he recognizes letter forms. Noble
and Noble.

Square-A-Shape—Perception game for one to three players. Geometric
shape cutouts on the square tiles guide the players in laying

down pieces to form larger squares or rectangles. 7G 146, $2.75, Childcraft.

Flannel Board Fractional Parts—Circles and squares including wholes, halves, thirds, quarters, fifths, sixths, and eighths. Also rectangles in wholes, halves, quarters, and eighths. Color coded. No. 7807, $3.00, Novo Educational Toy and Equipment Co.

VISUAL CONCEPTUALIZATION

1. **Recognition**
2. **Discrimination**
3. **Matching**
4. **Memory**
   a. **Motor**
   b. **Visual**
   c. **Auditory**

Pre-writing Design Cards—These 22 designs, plus 10 blank cards for your own make-up, may be used for children in a pre-writing program to train them to see the small or little, tall and long, and the space between blocks. Color blocks may later be used in making constructions. The blocks are placed on these cards to simulate correct size and spacing of what will later be letter formulation. Catalog No. P146, $3.00, Developmental Learning Materials.

Association Picture Cards I—These pictures help the child recognize a category, even though various items within a category may look radically different. The categories are: houses, chairs, tables, lamps, and clocks. Catalog No. P124, $1.00, Developmental Learning Materials.

Association Picture Cards II—These 30 cards of attractively illustrated trucks, birds, cars, dogs, boats, and hats are an effective and appealing way to help a child learn to re-group individual items into basic categories. There are 6 different categories with 5 different cards per category. Each card is printed in full color on strong tag stock, varnished and attractively packaged. Catalog No. P156, $1.00, Developmental Learning Materials.

Association Picture Cards III—This oversize series of picture cards is especially necessary for the child who needs practice in recognizing associations, categorization, and language development. They are beautifully illustrated and the series consists of 30 4" x 12" sturdy, varnished and easy-to-handle cards. On each card are four objects—one of which is not in the same category as the other three. The child is asked to select the wrong item and explain why that particular item is not associative to the other three and why the three belong in the same group. Catalog No. P157, $3.00, Developmental Learning Materials.

Sequential Picture Cards I—There are five sets of six cards each in this series. The child is asked to arrange them according to activity sequence. The series are: a boy sledding, a boy riding bike, going to school, a mother's daily work, and getting ready for bed. Catalog No. P127, $1.00, Developmental Learning Materials.

Sequential Picture Cards II—This series comprises the concept of very basic sequential patterning with 10 sets of 3 cards each. The cards are simpler and larger (6" x 5½") than Set I making them ideal for beginning practice in sequencing. The artwork is full of color and the subjects are most conductive to working with. They are printed on heavy stock, varnished and boxed. Catalog No. P161, $3.00, Developmental Learning Materials.

Sequential Picture Cards III—These are the most challenging and comprehensive sets of time sequencing cards available. Developed on a more advanced level than the first two series of sequence cards, these five groups of 6 cards each develop sequential thinking in terms of seasonal and 24 hour change, growth, production and daily activity. Catalog No. P162, $3.00, Developmental Learning Materials.

House Lotto—Colorful wooden lotto requiring visual discrimination on the part of the learner. Two boards (7" x 6½") have 12 houses differing only in small details. Houses to be matched are on 2" x 3½" boards. Catalog No. ACO6, $3.50, Lakeshore.

Sequence Cards—Excellent as a reading readiness activity. Cards are combined in groups of four, depicting actions in sequence. 80 cards. Milton Bradley Aids No. 7524, $1.25, Lakeshore.

Picture Lottos—Specifically developed as a pre-school, kindergarten, and first grade preparation for the learning of reading, the lotto stimulates the learner's ability to make accurate observations, comparisons and selections. *Ed-U-Card Lottos*—Sparkling and rich in color, these basic lotto games may be played by a group or the individual child. Each one contains six playing boards and 36 covering cards. Excellent pre-reading experience in noting likenesses and differences. $1.10, Lakeshore.

E100 *ABC Lotto*	E120 *What's Missing Lotto*
E101 *Zoo Lotto*	E121 *Go Together Lotto*
E104 *Farm Lotto*	E127 *Object Lotto*
E115 *World About Us Lotto*	

Picture Dominos—These dominos are an effective aid to the development of a child's perceptions. Twenty-eight colorful dominos, velour backed to prevent scratching or slipping, E102, $1.10, Lakeshore.

Visual Readiness Skills (for liquid duplication): Kindergarten Level I

1. Drawing within the lines
2. Tracing a pattern
3. Solving a maze
4. Completing geometric designs
5. Completing capital letters
6. Relating space and meaning
7. Relating space and form
8. Matching pictured objects
9. Noting detail is design
10. Recalling symbols presented

Visual Readiness Skills (similar to Level I only slightly more difficult): Kindergarten Level II

Seeing Likenesses and Defferences: Kindergarten Level I

1. Discriminating between pairs
2. Identifying matched pairs
3. Matching identical designs

Seeing Likenesses and Differences: Kindergarten Levels II and III

Visual-Motor Skills: Kindergarten and Grade 1 Levels I and II

1. Tracing a design
2. Completing a design
3. Sequence—reasoning, visualization

Visual Discrimination: Kindergarten and Grade 1 Levels I and II

1. External differences
2. Differences in size
3. Differences in kind

Independent Activities: Kindergarten and Grade 1 Levels I and II

1. Complete a design
2. Identify a missing part
3. Arrange ideas in order
4. Detecting absurdities

Complete sets, Continental Press Publications (Sample: *Seeing Likenesses and Differences* Level I, 25 dittoes exercises, $3.50.)

Animal Dominos—Matching colorful pictures of animals improves powers of concentration needed for reading. To develop perceptual skills, muscular coordination, and listening and speaking skills in young children, E103, $1.10, Lakeshore.

Jumbo Lotto, Community Helpers—Six extra-large playing boards with realistic drawings in full color of familiar community workers, and 24 extra heavy cards for matching, E1500, $2.25, Lakeshore.

On the Farm Lotto—Combines the fun of a jigsaw puzzle with the group play of a picture lotto. Each matching card shows a part of a farm yard animal. Can be played by one to four children, E550, $1.10, Lakeshore.

Around the House Lotto—Pictures can be put together like a matching puzzle by one child or played like lotto by groups. Large cards of various rooms in the house. Matching card completes room, E551, $1.10, Lakeshore.

Perception Plaques—Twelve pair of plywood plaques that have designs that appear similar but actually have slight differences, $2.75, Creative Playthings.

Let's Learn Sequence—An activity kit that leads children to ask themselves, "What happens first?" ". . . next?" ". . . last?" as they explore, manipulate, and identify the illustrations. Children build stories placing either three or six pictures in a sequence. Picture interpretation, inferential thinking and sequential order are developed. Includes pictures from nursery rhymes and every day experiences to build 10 different stories in proper sequence, 7L 245, $3.50, Childcraft.

Learning Lottos—These lottos are designed to provide exercises in visual discrimination. Each lotto consists of six background boards and 36 matching cards. Background boards measure 6" x 9", matching cards are 3" x 3", DE 603, $8.75 set, Creative Playthings. Three lottos:

1. Size discrimination
2. Size, shape, and color
3. Position

Twin Kins—Playing cards with boys and girls of different countries to match. Clothing colors are similar but not identical. Each card has a small design in the corner for matching, should the clothing be difficult. Arco Playing Card Co., Los Angeles.

SPATIAL PERCEPTION

Colored Inch Cubes—These one-inch cubes are assorted in six primary colors: red, yellow, blue, green, orange, and purple. They are made of finished hardwood. There are 96 cubes in each box. These are recommended for use with the programed design patterns listed below. Catalog No. W110, $4.00/box, Developmental Learning Materials.

Colored Inch Cubes Designs—Organization and spatial relation can be learned through building constructive designs with colored inch cubes. Thirty-four design cards are printed in six colors on tough tag stock and varnished. The patterns start with the very simple relationship of one block to another and graduate to complex diagonal relationships in diagonal patterns. In addition to learning simple and complex relationships the child learns sequencing, spatial perception and perception of foreground and background by focusing attention on the block design. This exercise in organization and space perception is intended as a preparation for spelling, working with numbers, reading, and writing. Catalog No. P111, $3.25/box, Developmental Learning Materials.

Spatial Relation Picture Cards—These are five series of pictures to demonstrate spatial relationships. There are six pictures in each series which demonstrate six spatial relationships. (1) On, (2) Under, (3) Left, (4) Right, (5) In front of, (6) Behind.

Catalog No. P125, $1.00, Developmental Learning Materials.

Space Relationship Cards—Each card has two space-relationship pictures and words. By drawing crayon lines, the child pairs up pictures with words. Cards have clear plastic laminations for easy marking with crayons, wiping off, and reusing; 35 cards. Milton Bradley Aids No. 7522, $1.50, Lakeshore.

Large Parquetry—This set of large parquetry consists of 32 blocks in the six primary colors. The shapes are square, diamond, and triangle. They are made of finished hardwood. The purpose of the large parquetry is to expand on the development begun with colored cubes. These blocks are large and easy to handle, but their various shapes and colors allow for more complex constructions. Catalog No. W113, $2.25/box. Developmental Learning Materials. Or Catalog No. P306, $2.15, Lakeshore.

Parquetry Designs (large)—Parquetry designs are an excellent way to teach organization and spatial relations. Twenty-two large design cards are printed in six colors on tough tag stock and laminated with acetate. Specifically, the purpose of using these designs is to teach the relationship of one form to another, visual sequencing, constancy of form in spite of color changes, matching color, matching form, spatial relation through the use of blocks in different forms and differentiation of background from foreground. These skills are a prerequisite for academic progress, and each skill can be identified in a specific learning process. Catalog No. P114, $3.75/box, Developmental Learning Materials.

Small Parquetry—The use of small parquetry requires more visual motor skill simply because the pieces are much smaller and harder to handle. There are four basic shapes including half diamonds. It is preferable to have the younger pupils graduate from large to small parquetry. Catalog No. W115, $2.25/box, Developmental Learning Materials.

Parquetry Designs (small)—Twenty designs for small parquetry are printed in six colors on tough tag stock and laminated with acetate. The procedure for use of these designs is the same as for the large parquetry, however, the designs are more difficult to construct. For example, a large square is made with four triangles and a large diamond is made with eight half diamonds. Other suggestions are made here to involve visual memory. Catalog No. P116, $2.25/box, Developmental Learning Materials.

Geometric Model Construction—Over 100 8" transparent plastic tubes with flexible joiners to aid in teaching the construction of figures. Teachers Manual, No. 7630, $3.50, Lakeshore.

Fairbanks Robinson Program/1: Perceptual-Motor Development—This program is listed under this category due to the large number of spatial relationships tasks. However, it includes tasks in fine hand-eye-motor coordination planning, figure-ground discrimination, form constancy. Complete program including instructor's guide, FR 1, $79.00, Teaching Resources.

BODY AWARENESS

People Puzzles—These puzzles, mounted on thick "super board," help the child recognize parts of the body and relate these parts to the whole. Many children put puzzles together by fitting the contours and do not see the content. Printed in full color, with water repellent coating, these puzzles are designed so that every piece is an essential, identifiable part of the person. The puzzle is assembled by organizing these identifiable parts into a whole rather than by fitting together uniquely contoured pieces. There are eight people puzzles: (1) Baby, (2) Sister, (3) Brother, (4) Mother, (5) Father, (6) Grandmother, (7) Grandfather, (8) Full boy on roller skates. Catalog No. P101, $4.50, Developmental Learning Materials.

Job Puzzles—"What is work? What is a job? What kinds of work, what kinds of jobs are these?" This is an ideal approach to body concept, vocabulary development, occupational recognition and visual and motor control. Eight job puzzles: (1) Mailman, (2) Nurse, (3) Teacher, (4) Fireman, (5) Football Player, (6) Farmer, (7) Policeman, (8) Painter. Catalog No. P100, $4.50, Developmental Learning Materials.

Animal Puzzles—The animal puzzles are also cut to separate different parts of the animal's body. The child can assemble front legs, rear legs, etc., helping to further build body concept. Eight animal puzzles: (1) Dog, (2) Cat, (3) Horse, (4) Cow, (5) Rooster, (6) Squirrel, (7) Chipmunk, (8) Deer. Catalog No. P102, $4.50, Developmental Learning Materials.

My Face and Body—Allows children to assemble large representation felt cut-outs for identifying and discovering relationships among major parts of the body. Includes 76 pieces, face features, total human figure, arm, leg, hand, and foot. No. 284, $3.95, Lakeshore.

Parts of the body on cardboard flash cards, 6" x 8", The Instructor Publications, Inc.

TACTILE DISCRIMINATION

Feel and Match—Twelve pair of scalloped discs of different thicknesses, backed with foam rubber. Tops of each pair are made from a different material. Children match discs which have like surfaces in discovering different textures. Catalog No. LR22, $2.75, Lakeshore.

Feel Bag—Bag contains eight different textures in commonly used pieces of material approximately 3" x 4" square. As the child reaches into the bag he will find materials that are furry, flimsy, fuzzy, rough, smooth, or silky. Recognition of the material or how it feels in the bag is designed to develop sensory perceptiveness. Catalog No. N621, $2.50, Lakeshore.

Giant Touch Numbers—Set of giant (7" x 11") black lacquer-finished cards with beaded numerals and dots provide visual tactile quantity concept for each number. Set contains 1 through 10. Catalog No. TK3, $3.95, Lakeshore.

Feel a Match—

    a.   Thickness—Fifteen 3-¾" rubber discs, five different thicknesses, five colors;

    b.   Length and Width—Eighteen rubber widths of 2", six lengths 6-½" to 2", three of each length.

Teaching Aids by Laurl Enterprises.

Touch Teaching Aids—Employing the tactile-kinesthetic method of instruction, these sturdy alphabet cards have letters that are coated with a pleasant-to-touch polished bead; the raised surface provides an additional sensory experience that speeds recognition of letter, promotes reading readiness.

      7L 240 Manuscript Caps $3.95

      7L 241 Manuscript Lower Case $3.95

      7L 242 Cursive Caps $3.95

7L 243 Cursive Lower Case $3.95
Childcraft.

Giant Beaded Number Cards—Each of these 7" x 11" cards represents
a beaded number with the corresponding quantity shown in
beaded domino dots. The visual tactile method of presentation
facilitates recognition of numerals, learning of quantity concept.
Numbers are pleasant to touch, on sturdy, heavyweight cards.
Numerals 1 through 10, 7X 173, $3.95, Childcraft.

Wonder Texture Box—This sturdy, wood box contains 24 pairs of
2" x 3" rectangles of cloth, fur, leather, synthetics, rubber,
cork, etc. DA810, $13.95, Creative Playthings.

Feely Meeley—Child places his hand in a box containing small plastic
animals whose pictures appear on the box top. His tactile discrimination is the only method to match the animals with the
pictures as he cannot see into the box. Milton Bradley Co.

Giant Plastic Dominoes—With dots in ¼" relief, 28 6" x 3¼" dominoes for see and touch tactile kinesthetic approach. No. G 104,
$6.95 set, Novo Educational Toy and Equipment Corp.

Klean Klay Model Clay Set—Four molds, six colors, tactile information to the finger tips, $.69, Art Chemical Co.

EYE-HAND COORDINATION

Lacing Card—Made of superboard and die cut into basic geometric
shapes and a free form, these lacing cards have been punched
with ¼" holes around all edges. Long lengths of colorful tipped
laces are included. The concept of shapes and forms is first
established by merely holding and working with the shape
itself. Actual lacing around the edges is a strong reinforcement
of the concept. In addition to gaining experience in muscle control, the child extends his sense of space because the lacing may
be done in an up-and-down fashion, or up-and-around or down-
and-around. Here the concepts up and down, in and out, over
and under are emphasized. There are five differently shaped
boards and five differently colored laces to a set. Catalog No.
P133, $2.50, Developmental Learning Materials.

Cuddly Kitty (Put Together Pet)—Children are intrigued by its
snap-on legs, button-on arms, a head that hooks on, a bright
red lacing and tying vest, and a shiny buckle and zipper that
opens and closes on his back. All of these six functions are in

one *Cuddly Kitty* that can help the child develop and improve his fine motor coordination for these everyday activities that are so necessary to establish a sense of accomplishment and self reliance. Catalog No. F155, $6.95, Developmental Learning Materials.

Pegboard Designs—This set consists of 200 pegboard design cards divided into two basic categories: overlays and pattern sheets. These are shipped in a sturdy "file" container with division sheets to make storage orderly and convenient. Catalog No. P150, $8.50, Developmental Learning Materials.

CANHC Tracing Book Puzzles (Book 101)—The purpose of the Puzzles Tracing Book is to provide a primary foundation in basic shape recognition and the proper method of line reproduction. California Association for Neurologically Handicapped Children.

Teaching Frames—These frames can be used for children in developing finger dexterity. The child learns to button his clothing before proceeding to the art of lacing his shoes, manipulating a zipper, or operating a snap-action fastener. Catalog No. AP14, Set 4 Teaching Frames, $11.50, Lakeshore.

Tinker Beads—Hardwood beads in six shapes and six colors for the child to match and string. Two strings included. Catalog No. TT300, $1.60, Lakeshore.

Sewing Cards—Eighteen cards and eighteen strands of multi-colored yarn, with plastic tips. Each card punched for easy sewing. Cute animals make set appealing to children. Milton Bradley Aids, Catalog No. 9383, $1.50, Lakeshore.

Pounding Bench—This pounding bench with nonremovable pegs for pounding has a set screw adjustment to tighten pegs that have loosened from wear and tear. Bench and Mallett, P125, $3.25, Lakeshore.

Creative Snap Blocks—Vari-shaped wood blocks, wheels, and rods in bright colors have metal snap fasteners permanently embedded. Parts are easily snapped together to make people, animals, trucks, etc. DR015, $4.25, Creative Playthings.

Threading Toys—A group of manipulative toys designed to incorporate the challenge of a puzzle. From a 7" square bottom comes: (1) single-bend wire, (2) four-bend wire, (3) spiral wire. Child threads small squares, triangles, and circles with a small hole.

> 7M 377 Single-bend wire—1-½ lbs., $4.95
>
> 7M 378 Four-bend wire—1-½ lbs., $4.95
>
> 7M 378 Spiral—1-½ lbs., $4.95

Childcraft.

Hammer and Nail Set—For ages 4 to 6. A liberal supply of sticks, dots, objects, blocks, nails, a hammer and board permit the creation of interesting designs. 7M 235, 2 lbs., $2.25, Childcraft.

Threaded Rod and Net Set—Extra-long threaded rod, 9½" x ½" diameter, comes with a dozen large unbreakable nuts in assorted colors. Appeals to love of repetition; encourages finger control and sense of symmetry. 7M 259, $2.10, Childcraft.

Doodle Blocks—A set of unstructured blocks, which permits an almost endless variety of combinations though it uses only two geometric shapes. Fifteen blocks. 7M 386, 5 lbs., Childcraft.

Play Panels—An approach to manipulative play using modern structural materials and design concepts. These 4" slotted squares of transparent polystyrene in brilliant colors interlock to form an unusual variety of appealing geometric structures, 30 squares in five colors. 7M 383, $4.95, Childcraft.

Lacing Shoe—The large holes and sturdy laces help shoe lacing. Figures of the "Old Woman" and "so many children" fit through slot in shoe and add interest. 7M 224, $3.00, Childcraft.

Workbench—Equipped with wooden claw hammer, screwdriver, nuts and bolts, and vise bench can be taken apart and put together again. 7M 224, $3.00, Childcraft.

Pipe Cleaners—Box of 100 12" pipe cleaners in assorted bright colors for a variety of projects. 2C 226, $1.00, Childcraft.

Metal Loom—An introduction to the basic principles of weaving. 7C 245, $.75. Jersey loops, 5 oz., packages in red, yellow, blue, green, orange, black, white, multicolor. For use with the metal loom. 7C 244, $.40, Childcraft.

Eye-Hand Coordination Exercises, Pathway School Program— Specifically related to unusual learning and perceptual problems. The materials are designed to help improve a child's eye-hand coordination by means of aids which involve the eyes and hands as a receiving, responding, performing unity. Materials include bracket and doweling to be attached to the wall from which hangs a ball (3" diameter) on a 3' string. Also included is a rolling pin type bat with three colored strips corresponding to strips on a 1' and 2' chart. Teaching Resources.

Rainbow Chain Strips for Chain Making—96 strips, ½" x 4½", gummed paper in eight brilliant colors for making chains, flowers, decorations, weaving, etc. No. 318, $.20/package, $2.20/doz. packages, Novo Educational Toy and Equipment Co.

Paper Sculpture—A source of ideas on how to transform a sheet of flat paper into scores of three-dimensional designs. Teaches how to cut, fold, bend, assemble, etc. $4.95, Novo Educational Toy and Equipment Co.

Hardwood Weaving Slats—100 slats 10" long in six assorted colors. No. 301, $.90, Novo Educational Toy and Equipment Co.

Craft Stix (popsicle sticks)—4-½" long, 3/8" wide, pack of 1,000, $1.95, Novo Educational Toy and Equipment Co.

Kikit—Within a 12" x 29" x 3" open box balls are "kicked" by movable paddles. The object being to paddle the ball to the opponent's goal. Higher level of eye-hand coordination. TK 4, $6.95, Novo Educational Toy and Equipment Co.

Popit Counters—Large, unbreakable, pliant, plastic beads pop into each other to form chains. Set of 20, yellow and orange, NN162, $1.75, Creative Playthings.

Frame Mosaic—This designing frame requires good eye-hand coordination. The plastic frame, 7" by 7" is divided into 169 ½" compartments, into which the child places the hardwood blocks. Blocks cut into triangles, rounds, and squares. BH 1405, $4.25, Lakeshore.

Peg Graded Board—A manipulative activity for the pegboard beginner that also provides training in relative size discrimination. Extra-thick pegs are easy to grasp, come in six graduated sizes. Identifiable by color, 30 pegs, 7M 293, $4.25, Childcraft.

Peg Activity Box—Durable plastic pegboard and pegs are excellent for creating free form and geometric designs. Pegs can be used with pegboards to form colorful patterns and combinations in the tray. 7M 294, $2.50, Childcraft.

Bolt Box—Bolts arranged on lid of box in sequence. Child fits nuts. Eight sizes form ½" bolt to 1/8". 405G, $3.50, Lyndoncraft.

Dot-to-Dot Pattern Sheets—The time-honored game of connecting consecutive dots by straight lines to see a picture or design result. An excellent task of eye-hand coordination. Each package of dot-to-dot paper consists of 20 sheets each of 20 different designs. (F), No. P143, $4.00, Developmental Learning Materials.

Tracing Designs—This set of 20 heavy design cards presents a variety of exercises in copying shapes, strokes, letters, etc., for use with tracing paper. H, No. P141, $3.00, Developmental Learning Materials.

Jumbo Beads Colors and Shapes Games—A special set of the jumbo beads for three games. One game focuses on color, another on shape, another on form—both visually and haptically. Set consists of 48 drilled beads 1 1/8" diameter in six colors and five shapes. Two sets of cue cards and stringers. Four bags and instruction booklet. No. 596, $5.00, American Seating Co.

Small Wood Frame Chalkboards—Writing surface is washable. Claridge Grapholite. Green or black. GT 1824, green 18" x 24", $4.60, American Seating Co.

Dubnoff School Program—Sequential perceptual-motor exercises. The program is designed to develop fine-motor control, to orient the child toward starting and stopping points, and to inhibit perseveration. DS 1, $11.00, Teaching Resources.

BIBLIOGRAPHY

Books

Anderson, Marian H.; La Berge, Jean; and Elliott, Margaret E. *Play With A Purpose*. New York and London: Harper and Row, 1966.

Arena, John I. (ed.). *Teaching Through Sensory-Motor Experiences*. San Rafael, California: Academic Therapy Publications, 1969.

Ashton, Dudley, *Rhythmic Activities, Grades 5-6*. Washington D.C.: American Association for Health, Physical Education and Recreation, 1964.

Ayres, A. Jean, *Perceptual-Motor Dysfunction in Children*. Cincinnati, Ohio: Greater Cincinnati District Occupational Therapy Association, 1964.

Barsch, Ray H. *Achieving Perceptual Motor Efficiency*. Seattle: Special Child Publications, 1967.

Barsch, Ray H. *Enriching Perception and Cognition*. Seattle: Special Child Publications, 1968.

Braley, William T.; Knoicki, Geraldine; and Leedy, Catherine. *Daily Sensorimotor Training Activities*. Freeport, New York: Educational Activities, 1968.

Chaney, Clara M.; and Kephart, Newell C. *Motor Aids to Perceptual Training*. Columbus, Ohio: Charles E. Merrill, 1968.

Cherry, Clare. *Creative Movement for the Developing Child*. Palo Alto, California: Fearon Publishers, 1968.

Cratty, Bryant J. *Developmental Sequence of Perceptual-Motor Tasks*. Freeport, New York: Educational Activities, 1967.

Cratty, Bryant J. *Psychology and Physical Activity*. Englewood Cliffs, New Jersey: Prentice-Hall, 1968.

Cruickshank, William A. *Psychology of Exceptional Children and Youth*. Englewood Cliffs, New Jersey: Prentice-Hall, 1963.

Delacato, Carl H. *The Treatment and Prevention of Reading Problems*. Springfield, Illinois: Charles C Thomas, 1966.

Demeter, Rosa. *Hop-Run-Jump, We Exercise With Our Children*. New York: John Day, 1968.

Edgington, Ruth. *Helping Children With Reading Disability*. Chicago: Developmental Learning Materials, 1968.

Ellingson, Careth. *The Shadow Children*. Chicago: Topaz Books, 1967.

Espenschade, Anna S.; and Eckert, Helen M. *Motor Development*. Columbus, Ohio: Charles E. Merrill, 1968.

Frostig, Marianne; and Home, David. *The Frostig Program for the Development of Visual Perception* [Teacher's Guide] . Chicago: Follett, 1964.

Getman, G. N. *How to Develop Your Child's Intelligence*. Lucerne, Minnesota: G. N. Getman, 1962.

Glass, Henry. *Exploring Movement*. Freeport, New York: Educational Activities, 1966.

Graves, Leroy (ed.). *Learning to Move—Moving to Learn*. Physical Education Kindergarten Grades 1 and 2. Los Angeles: Los Angeles City Schools, 1968.

Green, Arthur S. *Physical Education Activities for Primary Grades*. Minneapolis, Minnesota: T. S. Denison and Co., 1963.

Hackett, Layne C.; and Jenson, Robert G. *A Guide to Movement Exploration*. Palo Alto, California: Peek Publications, 1967.

Haring, Noris G., and Whitehead, Mable B. *A Profile of the EH Child and His Needs.* Pleasant Hills, California: Contra Costa County Department of Education, 1964.

Helfenbein, Louis N. *A Guide for Perceptual-Motor Training Activities.* Cleveland, Ohio: Euclid-Lyndhurst City Schools, 1968.

Ismail, A. H., and Gruber, J. J. *Motor Aptitude and Intellectual Performance.* Columbus, Ohio: Charles E. Merrill, 1967.

Kephart, Newell C. *The Slow Learner in the Classroom.* Columbus, Ohio: Charles E. Merrill, 1964.

Leaver, John; McKinney, Bill; Roe, Elaine; and Verhoeks, Judy. *Perceptual-Motor Activities.* Pontiac, Michigan: Board of Education, n.d.

Monroe, George E. *Understanding Perceptual Differences.* Champaign, Illinois: Stipes Publishing Co., 1967.

Mosston, Muska. *Developmental Movement.* Columbus, Ohio: Charles E. Merrill, 1965.

Myklebust, Helmer R., and Johnson, Doris J. *Learning Disabilities: Education Principles and Practices.* New York: Grune and Stratton, 1967.

O'Quinn, Garland Jr. *Gymnastics for Elementary School Children.* Dubuque, Iowa: William C. Brown Co., 1967.

Radler, D. H., and Kephart, N. C. *Success Through Play.* New York: Harper and Row, 1960.

Rarick, G. Lawrence. *Motor Development During Infancy and Childhood.* Madison, Wisconsin: College Printing and Typing Co., 1961.

Roach, Eugene G., and Kephart, Newell C. *The Purdue Perceptual Motor Survey.* Columbus, Ohio: Charles E. Merrill, 1966.

Rowen, Betty. *Learning Through Movement.* New York: Columbia University, Bureau of Publications, Teacher's College, 1963.

Sloan, William. *The Lincoln-Oseretsky Motor Development Scale.* Chicago, Illinois: C. H. Stoelting Co., 1964.

Sol, Gordon, and Golob, Risa S. *Recreation and Socialization for the Brain-Injured Child.* East Orange, New Jersey: New Jersey Association for Brain-Injured Children, 1967.

Sutphin, F. E. *A Perceptual Testing-Training Handbook for First Grade Teachers.* Winter Haven, Florida: Winter Haven Lions Research Center, 1964.

Valett, Robert I. *The Remediation of Learning Disabilities.* Palo Alto, California: Fearon Publishers, 1967.

Van Witsen, Betty. *Perceptual Training Activities Handbook.* New York: Teacher's College Press, 1968.

Reports

Arner, Robert S. *A Rationale for Developmental Testing and Training.*

Read to the section on Binocular Vision and Perception, annual meeting of the American Academy of Optometry, Chicago, Illinois, December 13, 1965.

Proceedings

American Association of Health, Physical Education and Recreation. *Proceedings of Perceptual Motor Symposium. Perceptual Motor Foundation: A Multidisciplinary Concern.* Washington, D.C., 1969.

Occupational Therapy Seminar. *The Proceedings of Occupational Therapy Seminar, Perceptual-Motor Dysfunction, Evaluation and Training.* Madison, Wisconsin, June, 1966.

Articles and Periodicals

Ayres, A. Jean. "The Development of Perceptual-Motor Abilities: A Theoretical Basis for Treatment of Dysfunction." *American Journal of Occupational Therapy* (July 1963): 221-225.

Ayres, A. Jean. "Pattern of Perceptual-Motor Dysfunction in Children: A Factor Analytic Study." *Perceptual and Motor Skills* 20 (April 1965): 335-368.

Barsch, Ray H. "The Concept of Language as a Visual-Spatial Phenomenon." *Academic Therapy* 1:1 (Fall 1965): 2-11.

Carlson, Paul V., and Greenspoon, Morton K. "The Uses and Abuses of Visual Training for Children with Perceptual-Motor Learning Problems." *American Journal of Optometry and Archives of American Academy of Optometry* (March 1968).

Eisenburg, Leon. "The Management of the Hyperkinetic Child." *Developmental Medicine and Child Neurology* 8 (1966): 593-598.

Fisher, Ralph. "Formation of a Gross-Motor Program." *Ontario Association for Children with Learning Disabilities* (1966).

Frostig, Marianne. "Visual Perception in the Brain-Injured Child." *American Journal of Orthopsychiatry* 33:4 (July 1968).

Goldsmith, Carolyn. "The Use of Rhythmic Patterning for Neurologically Handicapped Children." *Academic Therapy* 1:2 (Winter 1965-66): 114-119.

Robbins, Melvyn P. "Creeping Laterality and Reading." *Academic Therapy* 1:4 (Summer 1966): 200-208.

Rolf, Ida P. "Structural Integration Gravity, An Unexplored Factor in a More Human Use of Human Beings." *Journal of the Institute for the Comparative Study of History, Philosophy, and the Sciences* 1:1 (June 1963).

Scagliotta, Edward G. "The Displaced Sense." *Academic Therapy* 2:1 (Fall 1966): 53-55.

Slocum, A. L. "Some Basic Motor Activities for the Neurological Handicapped Child." *Academic Therapy* 1:2 (Winter 1965-66): 109-113.

Smith, Hope M. "Motor Activity and Perceptual Development." *Journal of Health, Physical Education and Recreation.* Washington, D.C. (February 1968).

Other Sources (Activity Cards)

Cratty, Bryant J.: Learning and Planning: *Fifty Vigorous Activities for the Atypical Child.* Freeport, New York: Educational Activities, 1968.

Garmston, Robert; James, Jean; and Yeager, Allen. *The Segmented Demonstration Physical Education Program, Circuit Training, Body Management, Tumbling Movement Exploration.* Santa Rosa, California: Bellevue Union School District, n.d.

Volwetz, E. A. *Gross Motor Perceptual Training Activities.* Vancouver Public Schools, Department of Physical Education, n.d.

Unpublished

Capon, Jack. *Outline of Motor Perceptual Activities for Kindergarten and Primary Grades.* Paper presented to annual meeting of the California Association of Health, Physical Education, and Recreation, Sacramento, California, March, 1968.

Dubnoff, Belle, and Chambers, Irene. *Perceptual Training as a Bridge to Conceptual Ability.*

SENSORIMOTOR ACTIVITIES

POSTURAL AND BILATERAL
MOTOR INTEGRATION

A.   Activities to inhibit primitive postural reflexes

1. Activities to inhibit the tonic neck reflex

a) *TNR Tunnel.* Divide the class into two equal groups. One group leans against a wall, supported by one arm, their erect bodies at a fifteen to twenty degree angle out from the wall. The opposite arm is bent, with the hand on the hip. The head is turned to the side of the flexed arm, with the chin resting on the shoulder. The other half of the class walks (crouching but not crawling) through the "tunnel" of children leaning against the wall, without touching either the wall or the children. The crouching children try to get their heads as close to the outstretched arms as possible without actually touching them. The leaning children close their eyes, indicating whether they were touched by those moving through the tunnel. Alternate the group facing the wall.

b) *Coffee Grinder.* Have the child place one hand on the floor, the arm extended. The opposite shoulder and the head face the ceiling. The arm on the upper side of the body is flexed, with the hand on the hip. "Walking" the legs, the child moves in a circle about the extended arm. Alternate the arms. This is a strenuous position to maintain for more than fifteen to thirty seconds. On the command of the instructor, the child's feet face the door, chalkboard, clock, etc.

c) *Pushing Off Balance.* The children pair off. Child *A* assumes the quadrupedal position, turns his head to the right, places his chin on his right shoulder and his right hand on his hip. Child *B* attempts to push or pull Child *A* out of this position, which Child *A* tries to maintain. Then reverse the position of the arms as the child exercises the left side.

d) *Bipedal Stretch.* In a bipedal position with both hands holding an inner tube band, the child flexes his left arm, turns his head to the left and stretches the band by extending his right arm.

e) *Inner Tube Roll.* The child rolls in an inner tube "barrel" which has been fabricated by taping several car inner tubes together. The rolling movement will be initiated by the child's head and neck if the barrel is tight enough, or if the child's hands are tied together with a loop of Velcro or an inner tube strip. As the child rolls, occasionally call him so he turns his head.

2. **Activities to inhibit the tonic labyrinthine reflex**

   a) *Scooter Exercises.* A gradually sloping sidewalk or incline board (listed under Recommended Equipment) and a scooter board offers the necessary ingredients for several activities which may assist inhibition of the tonic labyrinthine reflex.

      (1) Lying prone, the child rides the scooter down the incline board into a stack of cardboard boxes. This not only gives purpose to the activity; but, as the excitation level is increased, so is body tension.
      The child may also ride through a "tunnel" of boxes, trying not to touch them.

      (2) Lying prone, the child slides down a carpet-covered incline on a piece of plastic material such as oilcloth for tables, holding the front corners of the material while sliding. The incline should be set to such a degree of angle that the child experiences a burst of speed.

      (3) Riding down the incline board with speed, the child attempts to touch as many suspended crepe paper streamers as possible. These are hung from the ceiling in the path of the child's movement and just above his reach while lying prone.

      (4) Lying prone on the scooter and coming down the incline board with speed, the child spins himself in slow circles by placing a hand momentarily on the floor. This can be done in alternate directions. This same slow rotating motion can also be initiated by reaching for a handle that is suspended from a rope.

   b) *Stomach Pivot.* Lying prone over a 16-inch utility ball so it pivots on his stomach, the child tries to spin as fast as possible while keeping the ball in his stomach.

   c) *Mat Roll.* Place several four by six foot mats approximately twelve to fifteen feet from the base of the incline board. When the child comes down the incline on the scooter board, he turns himself by placing a hand momentarily on the floor. As the scooter turns sideways, the child strikes the mat. He rolls off the scooter board onto the mat and keeps rolling.

d) *Beanbag and Hoop.* Suspend a hoop three feet off the floor directly in front of the incline board. Give the child a beanbag or half deflated ball. As the child accelerates down the ramp, he tries to throw the beanbag or ball through the hoop.

e) *Slalom Pick-up.* Place a line of weighted cuffs at one foot intervals on alternating sides of the child's path. As he accelerates down the incline board, he tries to pick them up. The cuffs should be in a straight line.

f) *Inner Tube Catch.* Lying prone on a scooter board, the child comes off the incline board and tries to grab a suspended inner tube with one hand.

g) *Propeller Spin.* Lying on the scooter board in a pivot prone position, the child is asked first to spin in one direction, then the other. Let the child tell you how much and how fast he would like to spin. Let him imagine that his body is a spinning propeller. Have the child keep the scooter spinning over a mark that is on the floor.

h) *Slide.* Slipping down a slide head first while in a prone position can assist the child in supporting the extremeties against gravity. *Note:* It is of paramount importance to let the child be the judge of how fast he wants to come down or if he wants to come down the slide at all. Insure that the drop from the bottom end of thes slide to the ground is not too great. A mat placed there could prevent injury.

i) *Scooter Whirl.* With his arms extended and his hands gripping the ends of a tow rope, the child lies prone on the scooter board and is whirled in circles by the instructor. The rope is doubled and thirty to forty feet long, with handles on either end. How fast the child is whirled depends on the child. Using a hoop instead of a rope can give the teacher more control, and facilitate muscle co-contraction.

j) *Scooter Train.* Two to four children lie on their own scooters, one behind the other. A sufficient length of rope is attached to each scooter so they are four to five feet apart. The instructor then pulls the scooter train around in a serpentine fashion. The children change from one board to another to experience the different speeds and motions at different points in the train.

k) *Swing.* Lying pivot prone on the seat of a swing, the child extends his arms, grasping with his hands the handles of a rope which has been threaded through the links of the chains supporting the swing seat. In this position the child is pushed at the rate of speed he desires.

l) *Upending.* The child pulls himself up the side of a concrete playground tunnel while holding onto the teacher's hands, then slides down the opposite side, catching himself with both arms. Another variation of this activity is rolling over a barrel or large ball into a handstand. This can be prolonged by having the child count from one to ten.

B. Equilibrium reaction activities

1. Basic equilibrium activities

a) *Net Spin.* From the ceiling, suspend a net-type hammock so that both ends have a common point of origin. Floor clearance should be approximately one foot. The child, sitting or lying prone or supine inside the net, reaches out to spin or swing himself.

b) *Platform Swing.* The platform swing is constructed of plywood (approximately 2½ by 2½ feet and ¾-inch thick) and is surfaced with carpet. Ropes from each corner are attached to a yoke, which by way of a single rope is attached to an overhead beam. Floor clearance is approximately one foot and wall clearance six feet. The various activities are:

(1) Lying prone or supine on the platform, the child can spin or swing, spin and swing at the same time, or push off a wall rhythmically, with either the hands or feet.

(2) Sitting, kneeling or standing, the child can swing on the platform.

(3) Crawl on and through the platform as part of an obstacle course.

(4) Play with another child using the above activities (provided the platform and ropes are strong enough).

c) *Tumble Tub.* Available commercially, these 2½-foot diameter metal or plastic domes are an ideal apparatus in which children can explore basic equilibrium exercises in a non-threatening manner.

d) *Large inflatable plastic balls.* These are listed under Recommended

Equipment and are particularly useful objects to elicit basic postural responses. While holding onto the teacher's wrists, the child pulls himself on top of a ball. Once there, the child is free to explore movement while still holding on to the teacher's wrists. Generally, the child's response on the ball is a good indicator of the level on which he is functioning. If the child is hesitant about moving on the ball, revert to activities in this same group that are developmentally simpler. Variations include lying prone or supine, with the teacher holding either the child's hands or feet. If the ankles are held, more independent movement may be elicited if the child's knees are bent in a prone position and the knees and hips are bent with the child lying supine. Developmentally higher equilibrium experiences include both sitting and kneeling on the ball.

e) *Barrel.* Self-propulsion in cardboard or plastic barrels helps the child explore equilibrium. The child climbs into a large carpet-lined barrel (cardboard shipping barrels are excellent) and propels himself by shifting his weight inside the barrel.

f) *Balance Boards.* The balance board is constructed of plywood approximately two feet square and ¾-inch thick and with a dome or wooden cube for a base (see Recommended Equipment). Lying prone on the balance board, the child must readjust his center of gravity as the teacher moves a five-pound weight from corner to corner on the board. Balancing activities may also be performed in the sitting, kneeling and standing positions, which are developmentally more sophisticated.

g) *Scooter Train.* The scooter train has been described previously in the Tonic Labyrinth Reflex section, item j), and is also of use in Equilibrium Reaction Activities. Higher equilibrium activities are demanded of the child if he is pulled on the scooter in a sitting position. Holding on to the ropes with one in each hand, the child is moved about by the teacher, who alternates the pulling force from one arm to the other. As force is applied to one or the other rope, the child must make an equilibrium adjustment or be pulled off the board.

2. Equilibrium activities in a sitting position

a) *"T" Stools.* The use of a single-legged stool requires balance simply to sit on. Variations while sitting include:

  (1)   Rolling a ball to the sitting child, to be kicked back to the teacher.

(2)   Playing catch with a ball (provided the child is reasonably
        proficient at catching and throwing). Doing this while on
        a "T" stool requires constant readjustment simply to
        maintain balance.

   b) *Sitting astride a Barrel.* Two children, sitting on a barrel
      and facing one another, try to dislodge each other from the
      barrel without using their hands.

   c) *Rocking.* Rocking horses, rocking chairs, swings, self-propelled
      seesaws, large wire spools and hoppity balls all elicit varying
      degrees of equilibrium reaction from the child.

   d) *Disc Swing with Spring.* A wooden disk twelve inches in dia-
      meter and 1½-inches thick is suspended by a rope through its
      center. A spring is spliced into the rope above the child's
      grasp. Sitting on the disc and straddling the rope, the child
      bounces and swings, stimulating the vestibular system.

   e) *One-Hip Sit.* Balancing exercises based on sitting on one
      hip provide a number of equilibrium activities.

      (1)   Have the child sit on one hip, first with his hands on the
            floor and later without any support. Alternating hips
            strengthens the balance.

      (2)   Sitting on the floor with his legs bent up to his chest,
            the child uses his hands to spin himself. Once he is
            moving, ask him to raise his arms and lean backwards
            so he must balance on his seat.

      (3)   Using the same position as above, have the child rock
            himself backwards until he reaches a point where he feels
            he will roll onto his back. Then have him extend his
            arms and legs and balance himself.

      (4)   Have the child sit with his legs drawn to his chest. Have
            him shift his body weight to one hip, then advance to
            the opposite hip. Next, have him shift his weight back
            and advance to the other hip.

   f) *Differing Chairs.* The child sits down on chairs of varying
      heights, descending slowly and without using his hands. A game
      like musical chairs could be devised, requiring the child to
      constantly change his center of gravity.

3. Equilibrium activities in a quadrupedal position

   a) *Cardboard Sled.* A piece of cardboard two feet by two feet, with rope handles attached, is an inexpensive, easily constructed balancing device. The child begins by kneeling and resting against his feet on the cardboard, then progresses to standing on the knees. The teacher pulls the child, starting and stopping frequently. Linoleum surfaces work best.

b) *Hand and Knee Balancing.* Beginning in the quadrupedal position, the child:

(1) Balances on three body extremities.

(2) Balances on two body extremities (the arm and leg on opposite sides).

(3) Balances on one body extremity (the knee).

4. Equilibrium activities in a bipedal position (static)

a) *Balance Board.* Not only is the balance board an effective apparatus for balancing activities in a prone position, but it is also effective in the bipedal position. These are some activities that may be performed while the child tries to maintain his balance:

(1) Simple calisthenics.

(2) Identification movements (for example, touching the knees or hips).

(3) Throwing and catching balls, rings, hoops, etc.

(4) Target practice with beanbags.

b) *Twister.* This is a commercially available game which includes a sheet of plastic with colored circles and a spinner. As a remedial tool, its value lies in maintaining balance in unusual positions and in increasing trunk rotation. The child flicks the spinner, moving the designated foot or arm to the colored circle designated by the spinner. Continue the game, placing the extremities on colors indicated on the spinner board.

5. Equilibrium activities in a quadrupedal position (dynamic)

a) *Skiing.* Equilibrium activities can be elicited from a child by having him ski down a carpet-covered incline board on a sheet of plastic. This maneuver is carried out first in a crouching position and then a standing position.

b) *Jump Board.* This is a board constructed of plywood about eight to ten feet long by 1½-feet wide and ¾-inch thick, which has solid wood endpieces roughly 1½-feet by 6 inches by 3 inches. The child jumps on the board, which stimulates the righting response.

c) *Mattress.* Walking, jumping, and exploring movement on a box-spring mattress (or trampoline) will elicit postural adjustments.

d) *Obstacle Course.* Walking on wooden cylinders or tin cans made as stilts over a course marked for each step requires a good deal of equilibrium adjustment. The child balances an object such as a ruler or book on his head while walking through the obstacle course.

e) *Balance Beam.* Balancing on a beam bipedally requires high levels of equilibrium response and should not be used at the beginning level. Walking on a beam, the child focuses on an object held by the instructor. By focusing on the object, the child relies more on tactile and proprioceptive input to balance than on visual feedback. If the child is able to balance while focusing on a stationary object, try moving the object up and down, right and left, and in a circle. Additional balance board and balance beam activities are listed in *A Motor Perceptual Developmental Handbook of Activities*, available from Perception Development Research Associated, Post Office Box 936, La Porte, Texas, 77571.

e) *Roller Board.* The use of the commercially available "Roller Board" requires a high level of equilibrium adjustments. It should be used next to a wall or other surface which the child can use for support. This activity is not recommended for those experiencing difficulty in this area.
in this area.

C. Activities to integrate the two body sides

1. Activities which emphasize body sides (Bilaterality)

a) *Pivot Spin.* Lying prone on a scooter, the child spins himself using both arms together. An inner tube band around the wrists will facilitate movement in the desired direction.

b) *Jackrabbit Start.* Lying supine on a scooter, legs and hips flexed, feet against a wall, the child straightens his knees and legs quickly, giving himself sudden acceleration. This activity may also be performed in a prone position.

c) *Surfboard.* Lying prone on a scooter board with legs, feet, head and shoulders raised, the child simulates paddling a surfboard by extending the arms forward then passing the hand along both body sides simultaneously.

d) *Dowel Twist.* Lying prone on a scooter board, the child grasps a 2½-foot piece of one-inch dowel stock, his hands shoulder-width apart. The teacher loops the handles of the pulling rope over the ends of the doweling until they touch the child's hands. With the other end of the rope the teacher pulls the child, attempting to get the loops to slip off the end of the doweling. The child attempts to keep the rope from slipping off the ends of the doweling by tilting it into the direction of the pull.

e) *Bowling Pins.* Riding down an incline ramp on a scooter or cardboard box, the child holds a large ball (ten to twelve inches in diameter), or cardboard tube, in both hands and attempts to knock down bowling pins set up in the line of movement.

f) *Plumber's Helper Paddle.* Seated or lying prone on a scooter board, the child "paddles" himself along the floor using a plumber's plunger as an oar. It is important that the child place both hands on the paddle handle. In addition to the conventional method of paddling, the child can push or pull himself along on the scooter using the plunger as a pole.

g) *Rafting and Rowing.* Two-handed activities while sitting or kneeling produce a desirable bilateral effect. The child can play rafting and rowing games, propelling his body forward or backwards with his hands.

h) *Inner Tube Games.* Inner tubes can be put to a multitude of uses. One is to figure-eight the band around the ankles. The child then moves himself around an obstacle course pushing or pulling his body with the legs while sitting on a scooter.

i) *Games in a Circle.* Sitting in a circle, have the children hand a large (ten to twelve inch diameter) ball to one another, using both hands, while:

   (1)   Facing into the circle.

   (2)   Facing alternately in and out of the circle.

   (3)   Sitting or standing in a single-file circle, handing the ball over their heads, under their legs, etc.

j) *Cardboard Box Roll.* The child assumes the quadrupedal position inside a large cardboard box, with the ends cut out. Facing the sides of the box, the child bunny-hops, "rolling" the box around an obstacle course.

k) *"T" Stool Catch.* While the child is sitting on a "T" stool, throw him a large (ten to sixteen inches in diameter) ball, which he must catch and return. Using a large ball means that the child must use both sides of his body to catch and throw the ball.

l) *Inflated Truck Tire.* Using an inflated truck tire laid on its side:

   (1) Two children straddle the tire opposite from each other and facing opposite directions. Springing around the tire, one child tries to catch the other, moving either forward or backward.

   (2) Use the same approach as above, only have the children sit on the tire with their legs to the outside, playing tag and moving left and right around the tire.

m) *Bilateral Circles.* With his legs astride an old automobile tire or partially inflated tube, the child jumps bilaterally in circles.

n) *Heels-and-Toes Walking.* Have the child remove his shoes so he can feel his feet "walking" laterally in a heels-and-toes manner. First the body weight is on the toes while the heels move laterally apart, then the weight shifts to the heels while the toes move laterally apart, and so on. Move until the legs reach the "out" position, then return. Can the child move both feet simultaneously an equal distance? A variation is to move both feet together outwards to the side, shifting the weight from heel to toe as in the previous activity.

o) *Hula Hoop Jump.* Moving both feet and arms together, a group of children jump through a series of hula hoops held in a vertical position several inches off the ground and several feet apart. Children holding the hoops alternate with those doing the jumping.

p) *Bunny Hop.* Playing follow-the-leader, have the children bunny hop forward and backward. This activity can be done following a rope course or a painted line.

q) *Kangaroo Hop.* Have the child hold something between his knees, then jump with the feet together.

r) *Chalkboard Activities.* Holding pieces of chalk in each hand, the child makes large circles (two or three feet in diameter) simultaneously with each hand. Synchronize movement in a rhythmic manner. Vertical lines and horizontal lines can be accomplished in a similar fashion.

s) *Two-handed Activities.* These bilateral activities include:

   (1) Using large blocks or carrying boxes which can be moved only by using both hands.

   (2) Rolling or playing catch with a large (sixteen to twenty inch diameter) lightweight ball.

t) *Clapping Activities.* The teacher claps out a pattern and asks the children to:

   (1) Tell how many claps were heard.

   (2) Clap the same pattern the teacher uses.

   (3) Play "Peas Porridge Hot" and similar games of the childrens' own creation.

u) *Tether Ball.* Suspend a tether ball so it is approximately shoulder height to the child. Using a two-foot length of one-inch doweling with three colored rings spaced equally, have the child place one hand on either end of the dowel and hit the tether ball with first one colored ring, then another, etc.

v) *Crepe Paper Streamers.* On a short piece of wood doweling, tack an eight to ten foot piece of crepe paper or plastic streamer.

   (1) Have the child imitate patterns made by the teacher, such as figure-eights, circles and the like, both laterally and overhead, using the dowel held by both hands.

   (2) Using two streamers or ribbon sticks, one in each hand, have the child synchronize the movements of both.

   (3) Have the children write letters in the air or spell their names bilaterally.

w) *Ring Toss.* Have the child stand with his feet in a fixed position. Throw him rings which he must try to catch with a piece of doweling held in both hands. Rings are thrown to the child so he must move to the left, right, high and low, forward and backward, all the while not moving his feet.

x) *Bleach Bottle Catch.* Plastic bleach bottles with the bottoms cut off make nice scoops for catching games. Using a whiffle ball or beanbag, several children can play catch while holding the scoop handle with both hands.

2. Activities which contrast body sides

a) *Flip-Flop.* Lying prone with the left arm flexed, the hand lying directly in front of the eyes, the left leg is flexed at both the hip and the knee, the right leg (which the child cannot see) is extended, as is the arm on that side. When, "Flip" is called out, the head is raised and turned to the side, the left arm and leg being now extended, the right arm is bent at a right angle at the elbow and the hand in front of the face is about six inches away. The right leg is flexed at the hip and knee. The extended arm and legs are not visible if the head is turned in the correct direction. If the child has difficulty coordinating both the arms and the legs, begin with the head and arms only. As the child becomes more proficient moving the arms, then include the legs.

b) *Rope Pull.* The instructor holds a rope which trails in a straight line down the incline board. Lying prone on the scooter the child pulls himself up the ramp hand over hand until he reaches the top.

c) *Slide Crawl.* Crawling up the front side of a slide, the child holds on to both sides and pulls himself up to the top using his hands.

d) *Wheelbarrow.* One child holds the legs of another, who "walks" with the hands along a marked route.

e) *Tetherball.* The teacher holds a tetherball in front of the child, who is lying prone on the end of a bench. The child hits the ball sideways to the right with his right fist, then lets the ball swing past him. He then hits it to the left with his left fist. Instructions can be varied, such as three hits with the left fist, two with the right, and so on.

f) *Foot Hop.* This exercise is used by Dr. Kephart in the Purdue Motor Perceptual Survey. The child hops twice on the left foot, once on the right, until told to stop. Vary the directions so the child hops three times on the right, once on the left, and so on.

g) *Tricycle.* Riding a tricycle or similar play vehicle provides reciprocal movement.

h) *Scooter Board Chase.* One child chases another on a scooter board, both using their arms in a reciprocal manner. This may be performed in the prone, kneeling, and supine positions.

i) *Commercial Toys.* Purchased with discretion, certain toys that are commercially available can be valuable remedial tools. One such item is the so-called "Scat Scoota," which is a four-wheeled scooter propelled by placing the hands on the pedals or standing on the pedals. The child must alternately push and release on each pedal in order to maintain forward progress. Another commercial toy is the "Twin Stick," in which the child propels himself by pushing on one stick and simultaneously pulling on the other.

j) *Steering Down a Road.* Two children sit opposite each other holding a hoop between them, as if it were a steering wheel. On the chalkboard, the teacher draws two parallel lines which serpentine around the chalkboard. Next, the teacher draws a line down the center of this "roadway," simulating a car driving along. The students, with their "steering wheels," turn in the same direction that the instructor turns.

3. Directionality activities

a) *Perception and Directionality Tasks.* The following are examples of motor tasks involving spatial perception and directionality:

Climb *on* a chair.	Step *out* of a circle.
Climb *over* a chair.	Creep *under* a table.
Go *around* a desk.	Stand *in front of* John.
Stand *behind* a chair.	Stand *in* a box.
Stand *to the right of* a chair.	Stand *to the left of* a chair.

b) *Visualizing the Space Behind.* Children occasionally have difficulty visualizing the space behind them. Activities which may improve their ability include:

(1) Walking backwards (looking occasionally around to get a general picture of their surroundings).

(2)   Throwing objects backwards to a visualized target.

(3)   Falling or sitting backwards on a trampoline.

c) *Pattern Hopscotch.* The child tries to match his feet, hands and knees to cutout patterns laid out on the floor. They should be arranged so the child walks forward, jumps, hops, walks backward, and crawls (separately or in combination).

d) *Building Directionality Concepts.* To build concepts of such words as *in, on, under, near, between, behind, away,* place two blocks of different colors on a desk. Move one so that it is in, on, under, near, or away from the other and have the child describe its position.

Another exercise to build directionality is to give each child a red block and a green block and ask them to follow these directions:

> Put the green block *in front of* the red block.
> Put the red block *on top of* the green block.
> Put the green block *behind* the red block.
> Put the red block *beside* the green block.
> Put the green block *under* the red block.

e) *Telling Direction.* Have the child tell you the direction which certain letters (*d, b, p, r, a*) face. This can be done with objects as well, such as a swimming fish, flying kite, speeding arrow, rain from a cloud, rocket taking off, etc.

f) *Map Directions to a Hidden Treasure.* Teach the child north, south, east, and west. Locate and mark the sides of the room. Generalize to the school layout. Beginning with the classroom, in which directions are labeled on the walls, give each child a page of directions that say, for example, that to reach the "Hidden Treasure" the child must go north to the clock, east three steps, west to the door, out the door two steps, south twenty feet, east three feet, west forty-five feet, twenty feet south, ten feet west, and so on. Ask the child to find the "Hidden Treasure" without the direction labels in the classroom.

D.   Left and Right discrimination activities

a) *Hand Tracing.* Trace several copies of a child's left and right hand on a piece of cardboard. Place it on the bulletin board, where the child can match his hands to the patterns. Label the patterns *L* and *R*.

b) *Left and Right Discrimination.* To teach left and right directionality in everyday classroom activities, have the children stand to the right of their chairs. Have the boys go out the right door, the girls out the left door. Ask the boys to put their crackers on the left side of their milk carton, the girls to put them on the right, etc.

c) *Turn and Tell.* Ask the child to name some objects on his left, then on his right. Have him then turn around to face the opposite direction and do the same again.

d) *Circle Jumping.* Explain to the children how a circle can be divided into halves and quarters. Review left and right. For those children aware of basic laterality but experiencing difficulty with terminology, try placing a rubber band on the right wrist. The following clues can help the child distinguish left from right:

(1) Tactile impression.

(2) Visual clue.

(3) Word association (red=right, etc).

Then, with a rope or chalk, a child makes a three or four foot circle and divides it into quarters. Start with everyone standing and facing the same direction. Give the children a direction and tell them to jump and turn in the circle, from quarter turns to complete turns. For example: Quarter turn to the left, jump. Three-quarter turn to the right, jump. Do this as rapidly as possible without frustrating or confusing the children.

e) *Rope Crawl.* The child crawls along a rope on the carpet. Position him so the rope divides his body down the midline. This may help him identify the right and left sides of his body, especially when crawling unilaterally with an arm and leg moving on the same side together.

f) *Quick Changes of Direction.* Using quick changes of direction involving left and right orientation, have the child go through a sequence of directions such as placing his left side against the wall, lie down on the right side, etc. A number of sequences are helpful, such as having the child run to the nearest wall and touch his left shoulder to its surface, pick up a ball with the right hand, place the ball in a box with the left hand, etc.

g) *Activities Involving Holding.* Place several objects around the room, including one which weighs several pounds. Have the child hold the weighted object with either hand, as long as he knows the name of the hand. As the arm becomes fatigued from holding the weight, tell the child which side is the tired side. Then have the child quickly pick up all the paper clips with the weighted hand and put them into a box held by the other hand. Then have him reverse the hands to pick up erasers with the unweighted hand and put them into a box held by the weighted hand, etc.

h) *Transfer of Body Part Identity.* Have the child transfer the Left or Right identity of his own body parts to the same part on another child while maintaining a stable left-right identity relationship outside of himself.

i) *Directional Movement.* Have the child learn to associate directional body movement by drawing a line

    (1)   Away from the body.

    (2)   Toward the body.

    (3)   Toward the right.

    (4)   Toward the left.

j) *Beanbag Relay.* Form three or four single-file lines (depending on the number of children). The first child in each line holds a beanbag, which is passed back according to the teacher's instructions (left, right, over, under, etc). This means that the beanbag must be passed from one person to another by using a designated hand. A judge should be chosen from each line to oversee the line next to their own. The winning line must have used the correct body side and sequenced the activity correctly, as well as being the first side done. The last child runs to the head of the line when he receives the beanbag Variations on this activity include giving each child two tasks to perform and going through the series twice, either back to front or starting at the head of the line again.

k) *Opposites.* Instruct the child to respond with the opposite direction than the one given him. For example, tell him to lift his right hand. He must lift his left. There are a number of commands that can be thought of readily.

E. **Activities to enhance the visual perception of a horizontal sequence in space**

    a) *Network.* Have the child use large kindergarten blocks or grocery store boxes to build a line or network of these objects according to a preplanned, horizontal design.

b) *Horizontal Sequences.* Have the children use various combinations of parquetry blocks, large and small beads, etc., to plan, copy or reproduce from memory horizontal sequences from left space to right space.

c) *Independent Sequencing.* Parquetry blocks, large and small beads, felt cutouts, small boxes. empty spools of different sizes, and beaded and unbeaded pegs can be used to construct independent activities in horizontal space by sequencing with:

(1) Various colors.

(2) Various shapes (keeping same color, if possible).

(3) Various sizes (keeping same shape, if possible).

(4) Combinations of shapes, colors and sizes in ever more complex mixtures.

(5) Matching a line of sequenced objects with an already prepared similar line of objects.

(6) Reproducing a sequence from a model.

(7) Reproducing a sequence from a design picture.

(8) Reproducing a sequence from a plan the child has verbalized.

(9) Reproducing a sequence from a model the child has made (or which has been made elsewhere) and dismantled. This is essentially creating a sequence from memory.

(10) Matching a line of sequenced objects with a similar line of objects.

d) *Sequential Picture Cards.* Have the child match sequential picture cards which are available commercially from a variety of educational materials publishers.

e) *Construct Sequence Cards.* Construct picture sequence cards by cutting simple cartoons in sections that can be reconstructed in logical order.

f) *Sequences of Shapes.* Have the child "read" sequences of shapes, such as "circle, square, rectangle, star, circle," etc. These can be read from a card depicting these shapes.

g) *Sequencing Line Designs.* Have the child trace a sequence of various line designs on a chalkboard, a carpet sample, or a piece of paper. Tracing can begin with the finger and progress to the use of pencils and marking pens. Tracing design sequences are available commercially from a variety of sources.

h) *Letter Matching.* Have the child arrange simple combinations of letters into a sequencing arrangement that matches a pre-constructed example. Progress from dissimilar letters and numbers to those which include a lot of *b, d, p, q* and *9, 6* combinations.

APRAXIA

A. Tactile function

"Protective Tactile" function

1. Basic tactile input activities

b) *Sensory Awareness of Body Parts.* An increased awareness of body parts and their names can result when the child names body parts being vigorously "dried" with a terrycloth towel, fleeceball or hand-sized carpet sample.

b) *Ball Roll.* Children often enjoy a large inflatable plastic ball being rolled over them as they lie prone or supine. If the child asks for more, exert a small amount of pressure on the ball.

c) *Erase the Chalk Mark.* Draw a design or letter on a carpet sample with chalk and have the child erase it with hands, forearms, and back.

d) *Tic-Tac-Toe.* Older children can play tic-tac-toe with the same carpet samples. Following the game, erase the chalk marks. Use soft chalk.

e) *Mat Bump Pull.* Lying prone or supine on a sheet of plastic, piece of carpet, inner tube strip or large beach towel, the child is pulled onto, off of and in between mats spaced about 1½-feet apart. Bumping off one edge and onto another provides the desired tactile stimulation.

f) *Body Rubs.* Using a washcloth, fleeceball, carpet sample or corduroy "tingle board":

    (1)   Rub off chalk marks or adhesive coding dots which have been applied to various body parts.

    (2)   Rub off flour or talcum powder which has been

sprinkled on body extremities until it is no longer
visible.

(3)   Allow the child to use fleeceballs as freely as desired to
touch, scrub or pat the body.

g) *Bear Hug.* If the child is agreeable, a bear hug provides touch
pressure stimulation.

h) *Piggy Back Ride.* The child is reliant on his carrier and thus
clings to his body, receiving tactile feedback from the chest,
stomach, legs and arms.

i) *Back Scratch.* Rest periods offer the opportunity to scratch or
rub the child's back.

2. Tactual activities which require motor planning

a) *"Drying Off" on Carpet.* The child imagines himself to have
just emerged from a swimming pool. Lying on a carpet
(which serves as a "towel"), the child imitates drying off
by bringing his entire body into contact with the carpet.
To facilitate maximum tactile input, the child is encouraged
to dry a specified area, such as the front and back of the
legs, arms, head, stomach, chest, back, sides and feet.

b) *Log Rolling.* Log rolling on carpet, mats, foam strips and
other textured materials supplies a desirable touch-pressure
input. Movement starts with the eyes, head, shoulders, hips,
legs and feet, in that order. Structure the rolling by giving
the child an object, such as an eraser, to hold between his
knees or feet. This object should be carried to a specified
point (end of the mat, etc.). Ask the child to keep his head
aligned with the edge of the mat as he rolls. By doing this,
the child is encouraged to roll straight. If the child will
permit it, place a cloth bag over his head during this and
other similar tactile activities. This will increase tactile
awareness.

c) *Upright Rolling.* Upright rolling along a wall gives good
tactile impression to the shoulders and back. The feet
follow a taped line approximately six inches from the wall
and paralleling it. The body is held erect, leaning against
the wall. As the child "rolls" onto a shoulder, the hands
are brought to shoulder level palms out to brace himself as
his chest faces the wall. Continuing, he rolls onto the other
shoulder, back and so on. Give the child a definite beginning
and ending point. This activity incorporates nicely into an
obstacle course.

71

d) *Shoulder Slide.* Lying supine on a piece of sheet or plastic, the child propels himself along the floor (which should be the linoleum type) by pushing with his feet. The child holds the front edge of the sheet or plastic so as not to slide off.

e) *Shoulder/Hip Walk.* This activity is a modification of the one above. Lying supine, the child rolls to one side so the weight of the body is on one hip and shoulder. Advance the other hip and shoulder by pushing with the leg on the same side. Repeat the procedure for the other side. The head should be held off the carpet.

f) *Incline Board Activities.* An incline board covered with corrugated rubber matting, foam rubber, carpeting or similar material can be put to several uses:

(1) *Commando Crawl.* The commando crawl can use the shoulder and hip walk to crawl up the incline board in a prone position and back down in a supine position.

(2) *Log Roll.* Rolling up and down the incline board can be enjoyable, provided the incline is not too steep.

g) *Barrel Rolls.* Rolling in large carpet-lined barrels offers a good deal of tactile input. The child propels himself by shifting his weight inside the barrel.

h) *Inchworm Crawl.* With the child lying on his side, ask him to move himself both forward and backward from one place to another, in inchworm fashion. Start on one side, with the legs bent and knees to the chest. Move the torso forward first, followed by the legs. Repeat on the other side.

i) *Sandwich.* One group of children lie on a mat in the prone position. An additional lightweight mat is placed over them, forming a "people sandwich." Another group of children log roll over the mat covering the first group. Children between the mats must lie flat with their heads protruding. Do not insist on participation.

j) *Hot Dog.* Wrap the child in a sheet of foam one-inch thick and three by six feet in size. Secure it with tape to prevent it from unraveling. Should the child object to being wrapped or tied, do not insist on participation. Next, lay out three or four mats four feet by six feet in size about ten feet apart from each other. Make this into an obstacle course game. The child rolls across one mat, stands up, hops to the next mat, lies down, rolls across it, and so on. A modification of this game is to see how far the child can roll continuously in one direction without the mat being secured with tape around him.

k) *Cardboard Box Activities.* Cut away the top and bottom of a large cardboard box. Lying inside, the child can log roll or somersault forward and backward, moving himself and the box to a specific destination.

l) *Hammock Swing.* One of the many values of the hammock or net tied up to a common pivot is the tactual stimulation received while spinning or pushing rhythmically off a wall.

3. Gross discriminitive tactile function

a) *Magic Sensory Box.* Collect in a box an assortment of real or pictured objects that can be easily grouped as to sense. For example, to touch (a bit of yarn, a feather, a piece of sandpaper), to smell (a sachet, a flower), to hear (a whistle, a picture of a musical instrument) and to taste (pictures of food). Label four small paper bags with pictures to represent touching, smelling, hearing and tasting. One or two children are to sort the objects and place them in the appropriate paper bags. To check the exercise, have the children empty the paper bags one at a time, and tell the class (or teacher) why they sorted the objects the way they did.

b) *Object Interpretation.* To coordinate the visual-tactual systems as a foundation on which symbolic interpretation and manipulation can be based, identify different objects by touching and handling:

something smooth (glass or polished wood)
      "   rough (sandpaper or board with hammer marks)
      "   heavy (bolt, small piece of iron)
      "   light (paper clip or crayon)
      "   soft (cotton or velvet)
      "   thin/thick (block of wood, paper, cardboard)
      "   shaped (square, circle, cube, etc.)

c) *Texture Interpretation.* Have the child place his hands into various substances, feeling their differences in texture. Later, see if the child can do this with his vision occluded. Add other substances as desirable. Some suggestions are:

Finger paints	Mixture of flour and sand
Clay	Wet sand
Mud	Flour-and-water paste

d) *Finger Painting.* The child can do finger painting with various granular materials (sand, IBM punches, corn, starch, etc.) mixed in with the paint.

e) *Skin Localization.* With the vision occluded, see if the child can accurately locate:

(1)   Being touched in two areas.

(2)   Being touched in two places simultaneously.

(3)   Discriminate the direction of a moving stimulus.

f) *Telling by Touch Alone.* With the child's eyes closed, put a soft material in his hand (cotton, sponge, clay, dough, plastic bag stuffed with old nylon stockings, etc.). Have him tell by feel alone if the material is hard or soft. Repeat the same procedure with rough/smooth, warm/cool, sharp/blunt, sticky/slick and other contrasting textures.

g) *Texture Cards.* A set of cards can be made with surfaces varying from rough sandpaper to smooth nylon. Some suggested materials are: rough fabric such as burlap, fur, satin, tweed, leather, suede, cotton, manila paper, glazed paper and cellophane. The child matches them for texture, not appearance.

h) *Body Part Touch.* Touch the child's body parts (beginning with sensitive areas such as the hands, cheeks, etc.) with the items listed below. Have the child identify the part with his vision occluded. Objects include:

> *Light touch* — feather
> *Rough touch* — ruler or piece of wood
> *Smooth touch* — glass or plastic
> *Cold touch* — ice cube
> *Wet touch* — wet washcloth

i) *Which Finger.* This game is played by having the child put his hands under a pillow. The teacher gently reaches in and pulls one finger. The child has to guess which one it is. This game is probably too advanced for a child under six.

4. Tactile form and object discrimination

a) *Grab Bag.* Common objects are concealed in a bag. One by one, the children put their hands into the bag and identify objects by touch. Good objects for this activity are: pencils, blocks, paper clips, forks, pegs, and erasers. As they become more sophisticated at identification, use objects with only slight differences, such as a ball point pen, pencil, and leather tool all of the same size.

b) *Shape Identification.* Paste different shapes (squares, isosceles triangle, etc.) cut from felt onto cardboard squares. The child feels and identifies them with his eyes open. Have him then close his eyes and repeat the identification.

c) *Stencil Cutouts.* Make stencil cutouts of a circle, square, triangle, diamond and rectangle. Children feel the shape and describe what they felt.

d) *Form Identification.* Have the child manipulate various three-dimensional forms in his hand, without looking at them. Then have him look at the form board, which has recessed shapes in it that correspond to the forms he has been holding in his hand, then find the correct involute of the form he has been holding. An alternate exercise is to have the child (with his vision occluded) feel the recessed shape in the form board, then identify correctly the three-dimensional form.

e) *Form Distinguishing.* Show the child two blocks of different but familiar shapes. Have him close his eyes and hand the blocks to him, first one and then the other. The child must guess which is which. If he cannot tell, he looks. With experienced players, more than two shapes can be used.

5. **Letter and number discrimination**

a) *See-and-Touch Identification.* Cut large letters and numbers out of sandpaper (or cardboard on which sand has been glued). Let the child look at the shape while he runs his hands over it. Later he must identify the letter or number by shape alone, feeling it with his eyes occluded. The teacher must correctly orient the shapes at first. Later on, the child can orient the figure himself with his eyes closed.

b) *Pattern and Cutout Identification.* Cut letters approximately four inches in height from heavy cardboard or oak tag. Give the child (vision occluded) a single letter or number to identify. Then have him become familiar with and identify both the letter and the pattern from which it has been cut.

B. Kinesthetic function

a) *Hammock Swing.* Suspend a hammock from a single point in the ceiling, about four to six feet from a wall and about six inches from the floor. Lying prone or supine in the hammock, the child explores movement by pushing off the wall with both the hands and the feet.

b) *Hammock on a Pulley.* Suspend a hammock from a pulley or pulley system so the child can pull himself up and down. The height to which the hammock can be raised can be restricted by tying a knot 2½-feet from the pulley where the restriction is desired. This gives the child three feet or so of distance to explore "ups and downs."

c) *Scooter Board Push.* Lying prone or supine on a scooter board, the child bends his legs in frog fashion, then pushes off the wall to a predetermined point consistent with his ability. Make the goal realistic. On a slick linoleum floor, children may perform the same activity sliding on their stomachs or backs.

d) *Wall Bounce.* Lying prone on a scooter board, the child pushes himself laterally from one wall to the other. He pushes off with one arm and leg, moves sideways to the opposite wall, where he brakes himself with the other arm and leg. If he can flex them rapidly, he will "bounce" himself back to his starting point. A hallway or narrow room would be the ideal facility, but if these are not available, a heavy table and a wall will do.

e) *Weighted Cuffs on Arms.* Place ten-ounce weighted cuffs on the child's wrists. The child propels himself on a scooter board.

f) *Pushing Back the Walls.* This exercise attempts to work with the proprioceptive impulses of isometric activities. The instructor will have to be imaginative to involve the children emotionally. Begin by posing the children the problem of how to enlarge the activity room. Ordinarily, following some discussion, someone will suggest pushing the walls back or pushing the floor down. Exhort the children to collectively move the wall back by pushing against it with both hands. An alternative is to have the lie supine with their arms extended above their heads on the floor, pushing against the baseboard with their feet. They may also attempt to push the floor down with their hands.

g) *Mountain Climb.* The child holds a twenty-five-foot rope which is tied to a stationary object. The child pretends he is climbing a "mountain," holding the rope taut. Then he rappels (backward movement) back down the "mountain."

h) *Floor Pull.* This is a variation of the previous activity in which are "fully inflated." Once inflated, they develop a leak and feet in front of his body, and attempts to pull himself along by using the rope.

i) *Pole or Rope Climb.* Activities such as climbing a rope or pole activate the proprioceptors. Hand over hand movements are suggested. For children unable to pull themselves up, pulling themselves along while lying on a scooter board activates the muscles, though not as strongly.

j) *Playing Balloon.* The teacher slowly blows up a balloon (preferably one with an image on it such as Mickey Mouse). The children lie supine and imagine themselves as uninflated balloons. The teacher blows up his balloon while the children pretend that someone is blowing them up as well. As the teacher's balloon enlarges, the children "expand" until they are "fully inflated." Once inflated, they develop a leak and slowly deflate and crumble to the floor. As they slowly deflate (with their eyes closed), the teacher has them stop periodically and hold a position for several seconds.

k) *Various Kinesthetic Activities.* The following activities give kinesthetic impressions resulting from moving the body into various positions. The child imitates the postures that the teacher performs in front of him. All these begin from an erect standing position.

   (1) Bend sideways from the waist, left and then right.

   (2) Bend forward and backward from the waist.

   (3) Rotate the body at the waist.

   (4) Extend the neck upward and rotate the head.

   (5) Bend the head laterally, left and then right.

   (6) Stand on toes, then on heels.

   (7) Rotate one arm in large circles, then the other arm.

   (8) Swing the arms to and fro to both sides.

   (9) Deep knee bends.

   (10) Flex and extend foot.

   (11) Bend ankles laterally in and out.

   (12) Bend elbows and wrists.

   (13) Flex and extend fingers and toes.

   (14) Rotate the arms in both directions and hold momentarily.

   (15) Lift the shoulders.

l) *Playing Deliveryman.* Have the children play Deliveryman, pushing a loaded cart, wagon or wheelbarrow to and from a specific location. A heavy object (or another child) in the cart will supply the proper proprioceptive input.

m) *Wing Flap.* Lying pivot prone with their arms flexed and parallel to the floor and the hands directly in front of the face, have the children imagine these are "wings" that they can flap. Stretch an inner tube between their hands and have them flap their "wings."

n) *Peg Leg.* Most children have seen pictures of pirates with wooden legs. The teacher can ask them to simulate having a pegleg by walking with an inner tube strip stretched between both hands and feet. The stiff-legged walking that results causes co-contraction and joint compression. Have the children walk around the inside of a rope circle, avoiding contact with all the others.

o) *Rock-a-Baby.* Two children sit opposite one another, their legs extended and feet touching. Each one holds an end of an inner tube strip stretched between them. Keeping the arms and legs extended, they rock back and forth.

p) *Scooter Pull.* This activity requires a three to four foot piece of inner tube strip approximately 2½-inches wide. The teacher holds one end of the strip in each hand. With his legs spread apart about three feet, he leans forward and gives the child the center of the strip. The child is lying prone on the scooter board. He grasps the strip with his hands ten to twelve inches apart and arms extended. The teacher then moves the child in a shuttlecock fashion while the child holds his arms extended.

q) *Scooter Whirl.* Positioned prone on the scooter board, the child holds onto a strip of inner tube six to eight feet long and 2½-inches wide. His arms are extended and he holds the tube with both hands. The instructor whirls the child around him in circles, alternately pulling hard on the strip for more speed and easing tension to slow the child.

r) *Inner Tube Bounce.* Two children sit ten to fifteen feet out from the end of an incline board, holding a long inner-tube strip between them so it stretches across the path leading from the incline board. A child coasts down the board into the "barrier" and is slowed to a halt. All of the children receive co-contraction of the arm muscles.

s) *Wheelbarrow.* One child "walks" on his hands, with his feet being held by a partner. The kinesthetic features of this activity are joint compression and co-contraction of the arms and knees. A variation of this has the child holding on to an exercise wheel, following a rope strung in a serpentine fashion across the floor. The child should follow the rope as closely as possible without touching it.

t) *Tandem Inner Tube Bounce.* Fasten a long (more than ten feet) inner tube strip about 2½-inches wide to two walls, held off the floor about six inches. Two children, lying prone on scooters are on opposite sides of the inner tube, facing each other. Their hands are spaced about one foot apart, and are separated from each other about two feet. Methods of movement include:

   (1)   Move together and apart in a continuous rhythm.

   (2)   Lie on the same side of the strip and move forward in tandem.

u) *Under-the-Teacher Bounce.* The teacher holds the ends of a shorter inner tube strip (four feet long and 2½-inches wide) and spreads his legs about three to four feet apart. He leans forward and gives the child, who is lying prone on a scooter, the strip. As the child is pulled toward the teacher, he releases the strip as he glides under the teacher. The child's legs should be bent upwards at the knee. The teacher now loops the inner tube strip against the child's legs as they pass beneath. Pulling on the strip to stop the child's momentum and begin accelerating the child back the other way, the teacher releases the strip from the legs as they pass under and holds the strip for the child to grasp again. Shuttling back and forth in a rhythmic manner, co-contraction of the arms and the legs is provided.

v) *Playground Bars.* Hanging and moving on playground bars activates the proprioceptors. Incorporate these activities in a bars obstacle course.

w) *Hot Potato.* Have the children play catch at close range with a medicine ball (children's size) or heavy beanbags.

x) *Ping Pong Golf.* One of the most appealing games for children is to have them get into the quadrupedal position and then blow ping-pong balls (or 3" by 5" sheets of paper) around an obstacle course or to a given destination. This is preferably done timed and with others in a relay. The child receives co-contraction of the back and neck muscles.

79

y) *Scooter/Hoop Activity.* Having children move lying prone on a scooter board while holding hoops in the hands at a spacing of approximately shoulder-width apart is an excellent method of bringing about co-contraction of the arm muscles.

z) *Tracing.*

C. Gross motor planning activities

1. In the prone and supine positions

a) *Turn the Head toward a Sound.* Lying supine with the eyes closed, the child is asked to turn his head toward a sound. These should alternate from left to right to stimulate head movement from one side to the other.

b) *Roll Over.* Lying supine, the child begins to roll over first by turning the head, then the shoulders, arms, hips and finally, the feet. Ask him to keep his head aligned on the mat edge where he is rolling.

c) *Cardboard Box Roll.* Cut away the top of a heavily constructed cardboard box. Place the box on its side and have the child enter feet first. The child pushes against the side of the box to get it rolling. He can also propel the box while in a quadrupedal position, crawling sideways against the side of the box. Alternatively, he can face the sides of the box and roll it by crawling forward or backward. These same methods of movement work also with a heavy cardboard barrel.

d) *Scooter Board Tag.* Two children ride scooter boards, either prone, supine, or sitting. One child has a ten-foot length of string trailing behind him. The other child tries to catch the string while the child tries to elude him.

e) *Scooter Board Crawl.* Lying prone on a scooter board, the child tries to pull himself along a 25 to 50-foot length of rope that is tied tautly so that it is about six inches to one foot off the floor. This can also be done supine, kneeling and sitting. In the sitting position, the child should sit with his legs crossed, Indian style. He can then pull himself hand over hand forward or hand sliding over the other sideways. These positions are developmentally more advanced than the simple prone and supine positions.

f) *Serpentine Course.* The child lies prone on a scooter board and follows a painted line (or piece of rope) by keeping the line in between his scooter's wheels.

g) *Obstacle Course.* Lying prone or supine on a scooter board, the child moves his body over, through, around, and under various obstacles. Using both hands together (bilaterality) or one and then the other (contrasting body sides), the child moves through the obstacle course. Tell him to move from one manner of pulling to the other in quick succession.

h) *Rolling Sit-up.* The child lies prone, hands on the ground next to his shoulders in the push-up position. To roll to the right, have him extend the right arm while the left arm is flexed. As he approaches the sitting position, extend the left arm and sit upright. Once the child understands how to arrive at this position, ask him to assume it first right and then left, mixing the two. For the child with laterality difficulty, tell him what his eyes should see if he is sitting in the correct position. Tax the motor planning ability by asking him to sit up, changing sides quickly.

i) *Angels in the Snow.* Ask the child to lie on his back, arms to the sides, legs and feet together. Slide both extended arms simultaneously over the head until the hands touch, then back to the side. Be sure he moves them along the floor or mat. Next, the child slides his legs laterally through their full range of movement, heels touching the floor. Once the children have learned what to do, tell them to:

(1) Move just this arm (point to left arm) and back.

(2) Move just this arm (point to right arm) and back.

(3) Move just this leg (point to left leg).

(4) Move just this leg (right leg).

(5) Move both arms.

(6) Move both legs.

(7) Move this arm and leg (point to left arm and left leg).

(8) Move this arm and leg (point to left arm and right leg).

(9) Move this arm and leg (point to right arm and left leg).

(10) Move this arm and leg (point to right arm and right leg).

2. In the quadrupedal position

a) *Commando Crawl.* Lying prone with his head and shoulders up, the child propels himself by using his cross-lateral elbows and knees.

b) *Creeping Exercises.* There are several positions in which creeping can be useful.

(1) Arms and legs moving as separate units. The arms move together, the legs follow together in bunny-hop fashion (either forward or backward, or both).

(2) Using the left and right body sides independently. In the quadrupedal position, move first with the left side (hand and knee), then the right side (hand and knee).

(3) Cross-lateral crawling. Left hand moves with the right knee, the right hand with the left knee. Move forward and backward.

As proficiency is gained creeping forward, stress moving backward and sideways (as in item 2 above). Have the child change rapidly from one method of creeping to another. For example, have him bunny hop forward, move backward by moving first one body side and then the other, move left or right as instructed using one side of the body, then slide the other side to it.

c) *Checkerboard Patterns.* One-foot squares are painted on the blacktop or cafeteria floor. Two children in the quadrupedal position play tag while placing their hands only in white squares. Later they must keep both arms and knees in the dark squares.

d) *Crab Walk.* Ask the child to squat down, reach backward and put both hands on the floor behind him without sitting down. Have him walk or run in this position. He should keep his head, neck and body in a straight line.

e) *Commercially Available Equipment.* Several manufacturers of educational materials make patterns of hands or feet (paper cutouts are not durable enough) which are useful in a variety of ways. One such way is an obstacle course where, in addition, to going over, under, around, and through, the children must pattern their feet, hands, and knees to conform with plastic or rubber cutouts placed by the teacher. These can be set up so the child walks, hops, jumps, crawls, turns, etc., going forward, backward, sideways and so on.

3. In the bipedal position.

a) *Toy Soldier Walk.* The child walks stiff-leggedly forward, pointing to the left foot with the left hand and the right foot with the right hand.

b) *Oversized Shoes.* Large shoes made out of shoeboxes can be worn as the child follows a string laid out in a serpentine fashion. Swimfins and snowshoes also work well.

c) *Fast and Slow Walking.* Using imaginary situations such as crossing a desert on a hot day or pulling a loaded wagon that has square wheels, have the child increase or decrease his pace.

d) *Puddle Hop.* Have the children pretend they are walking or running over puddles of decreasing and then increasing size. Caution them on trying this approach on the real thing.

e) *Mirroring Hop.* Have the children stand opposite a partner and hop or jump in rhythm to the pace set by the partner. It may help them if they hold hands. This activity can be performed with either the right or left foot forward, or side by side, moving forward or backward.

f) *Sideways Walk.* Have the children stand opposite a partner and then begin to walk sideways, keeping foot to foot while crossing one foot in front or behind the other, keeping in step and pacing one another.

g) *Musical Hop.* With the teacher playing on a piano, guitar, or other suitable musical instrument, have the children hop to fast chords, jump to slower chords and walk to moderate chords. Shorter or longer intervals can be added for skipping, galloping, or sliding.

h) *Non-Locomotive Movements.* Movements which do not involve motion from place to place, such as twisting, swaying, bending, swinging extremities, extending and contracting can have many possibilities for rhythmic movements. Pushing, pulling, dodging and falling are other activities than can be used to strengthn rhythmic patterns.

i) *Breaking Music into Basic Beats.* Another way to use the rhythmic approach in Gross Motor Planning is to break music into its component beats. For example, expose the children to a basic 4/4 drum beat, accenting the first beat in the measure. Children will enjoy walking to the rhythm, clapping the accent as they go. In a more advanced movement, combine a twist or thrust on the accent with walking in the rest of the measure. In a similar manner, 2/4, 3/4, 3/8 and other beats may be used.

j) *Voice Commands.* Have the children perform jumping,

hopping, and other sequences to their own voices. For example, jump/hop/jump/jump/hop/hop and so on.

k) *Body Alphabet.* Lying on a carpet, the children try to make with their own bodies the following letters and numbers from the teacher's chalkboard models: *1, 5, 6, 7, L, S, C, J, O, U, V.* With a partner they can make *8, 9, 4, 3, 2, X, A, E, F, K, H.* On a sunny day outside they can make numbers and letters with their shadows, either individually or with partners. Groups can attempt simple words.

l) *Imitating in a Mirror.* Using a large mirror, the children try to imitate the movements of their teacher while watching their own images. A variation of this activity would include a strip of paper with postured drawn on it, or five-by-eight-inch cards with postures drawn on it.

m) *Mirroring with Hoop.* Each child holds a hoop in front of his body with both hands. The teacher says, "Make your hoop like mine," and the children try to mirror the position of the teacher's hoop.

n) *Name Game.* Hearing their own names as a part of a movement game is appealing to many children. For example, the teacher can say, "Mary Jones, jump, jump, hop, hop." Also, the teacher can clap out a rhythm and the children respond with various types of movement.

o) *Quick Posture Changes.* Rapid changes of posture aid in good motor planning. Some examples are:

  (1) Standing.

  (2) Kneeling.

  (3) Sitting cross-legged.

  (4) Sitting knee bend, feet flat on the floor.

  (5) Squatting.

  (6) Lying on side.

  (7) Lying on stomach.

  (8) Lying on back.

p) *Simon Says.* This time-tested game has considerable value as a motor planning activity. The teacher's directions should include a variety of gross motor movements, such as hopping, jumping, leaping, crawling, sliding, galloping, etc. Later, precede the type of movement with the following: quick, slow, jerky, fast, graceful, etc.

q) *Treasure Hunt.* Make a graphically illustrated map describing how to find a "hidden treasure." Make it so that the child begins in the classroom and follows a path to arrive at the next "clue." Use a minimum of fixed objects on the map from which the child can relate spatially.

r) *Follow the Posture.* The child imitates a simple posture performed by the teacher. The teacher has the child hold that posture while he himself goes on to another one. The teacher then assumes a third one while having the child try to imitate the second. The teacher is always one posture ahead of the children. More than a two-posture spread between the teacher and children is usually too difficult for primary children.

D. Fine motor planning. Eye-hand coordination activities

a) *Woodworking.* Nails and scrap lumber can be used for motor planning tasks that emphasize the use of a single hand for skill and the other hand for helping and holding. Small hand tools can be used for pounding, sawing and screwing. Construction of specific, planned woodworking projects adds a dimension of form and space awareness.

b) *Painting.* Various forms of painting useful in motor planning are:

   (1) Finger painting.

   (2) Easel painting.

   (3) House painting ("painting" with a large brush and a can of water on the sidewalk, patio, etc.).

c) *Yarn Games.* Yarn or simple string offers many possibilities for training in fine motor planning. The teacher wraps a short segment of yarn around pegs in a pegboard, making a design. The child, whose pegboard is set up in an identical fashion, imitates the teacher's design.

d) *Object Sorting.* Have the children sort various small objects such as paper clips, rubber bands, etc., into small boxes.

e) *Knot Tying.* Tying simple knots (overhand, square, granny) can be a valuable experience. The teacher ties several overhand knots at one-foot intervals along a length of rope. The rope is then strung on the floor and the child attempts to tie knots in his rope to match the spacing of knots in the teacher's rope.

f) *Puppets.* Hand and finger puppets can be used not only to tell a story but involve motor planning and conceptual sequencing. Children with the puppets make them ini-imitate such gestures as swimming, skating, playing hop-scotch or acting out simple stories. The other children try to guess what the puppets are doing.

g) *Finger Games.* Activities with the fingers include:

   (1)   Putting clothespins around a shoebox to tell time.

   (2)   Putting clothespins around a shoebox following a pattern made up by the teacher. The child checks his arrangement against the model.

   (3)   Finger races are also fun.

h) *Stringing Beads.*

i) *Making Macaroni Bracelets.*

j) *Snap Together Beads.*

k) *Sewing Cards.*

l) *Practice Buttoning, Zipping and Lacing.*

m) *Looper Looms.*

n) *Construction Toys.* (Tinker Toys, Lincoln Logs, etc.)

o) *Fitting Nesting Toys Together.*

p) *Making Paper Ring Chains.*

q) *Paper Folding.* Primary art books often include objects constructed from simple paper folding techniques. Paper folded in an accordian pattern makes a fan, etc.

r) *Making a Folded Paper Basket.* Fold a sheet of 8½ by 11-inch paper the long way. Fold it in half again. Now unfold it and fold it in half the short way. Fold in half again, as was done the long way. Unfold it and there will be six creases (see fig. 1). Next, fold along the creases as shown in fig. 2. Then fold the corners over as in fig. 3. Now fold over the center tab and as in fig. 4, and pull the basket into shape.

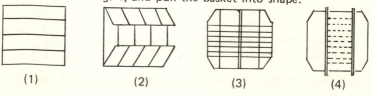

(1)   (2)   (3)   (4)

s) *Magazine Tear-Outs.* The children tear pictured objects such as a ball, tree or house from a magazine or newspaper.

t) *Coloring in Stencils.* The first stencil should be a piece of heavy cardboard about six inches square, out of which a four-inch square has been removed, leaving a one-inch thick frame. The child colors inside the frame. The instructor should make certain that the entire square is filled in. Variations of this activity include:

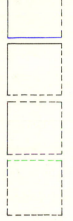

(1) Making a square template with one side removed. Substitute a heavy black line for the missing side. Have the child color within the square.

(2) Use a template with only two sides, again substituting heavy lines for the missing sides.

(3) Use a template with three heavy lines and only one solid side.

(4) Finally, the child colors within a square of heavy lines only.

u) *Geometric Drawings.* With crayons, outline geometric templates to make various designs.

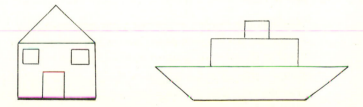

v) *Coloring Exercises.* Have the children color inside simple forms outlined in heavy black lines. This can progress to simple coloring books. Be sure the child understands the various parts of the pictures he is about to color, so he does not, for example, color one sleeve of a shirt blue and the rest of the shirt red. The teacher can avoid this kind of disassociation by outlining the separate elements in the picture with the color the child is to use in that part of it.

w) *Follow the Dots.* Commercial follow-the-dots books can be colored using crayons or marking pens.

x) *Tracing.* Trace over large designs, shapes and letters, first with the finger only, next with tracing paper and crayons, and finally, giving the child a new piece of paper and having him reproduce the design from memory. This new design is then checked against the master. Once larger designs are mastered, the child can progress to smaller designs.

y) *Freeflowing Designs.* Working left to right on a large sheet of paper, the child makes a freeflowing design such as this:

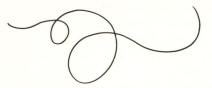

The next step is to trace over this free movement, and if he makes errors, trace along the line marking where his errors were made.

z) *Sand Serpent.* On a large piece of construction paper, make a serpentine trail with glue, then sprinkle sand over it. When the glue has dried, the child follows its course with a finger, then tries to duplicate the pattern on the table top with his vision occluded. Finally, the child duplicates from memory the pattern on a piece of paper using a crayon.

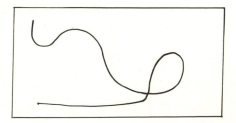

aa) *Dot Game.* Give the children sheets of paper with a generous left margin left blank (see diagram, next page), and clusters of squares, circles and triangles drawn on the right hand section. Direct the children to start at the margin and put a dot in each circle or triangle or square that he finds. Combinations of these shapes can also be used. Have the child place dots in the indicated shapes as quickly as possible.

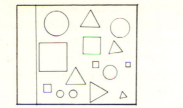
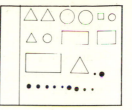

bb) *Line Game.* A variation of the above activity is to give the children sheets of paper with vertical lines arranged in groups of different numbers of lines per group (see diagram). Have the children start at the margin and draw a horizontal line through the center of each cluster of (for example) two lines. Repeat with clusters of three lines, four lines, etc.

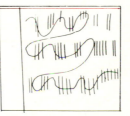

cc) *Clock Game.* In this activity, both sides of the body are oriented independently, but must perform directional movements simultaneously. Have the child place his right hand on one of the numbers and his left hand on another. The teacher calls out new numbers, and the child moves both hands simultaneously to those number.

dd) *Dot Chase.* Place a dot on the chalkboard and have the child place his piece of chalk on it. Place another dot randomly on the board and have the child draw a line from the first dot to the second dot without lifting the chalk. Place a new dot and have the child connect to this one. Make it a game, with the child drawing to each randomly placed dot in chase of the teacher's own chalk. If the child has difficulty drawing straight lines or maintaining directionality, make the distances shorter, then gradually increase them. If the child has difficulty stopping at any of the dots, guide his hand or place an eraser on each dot so he bumps it and stops. Also, the teacher can chant a rhythmic phrase, such as, "Hit the dot," with the marked accent on the last word. The rhythm helps to maintain attention. Increase the speed of placing the dots and decrease the time the child remains on each one. Place the dots so that several of the lines have to be crossed and recrossed.

ee) *Flashlight Tag.* The child must follow the teacher's flashlight, which is being projected on a wall, with his own flashlight. Teachers should make large motions. In addition to holding the flashlight in his hands, the child can also hold it under his arms.

ff) *Line Tracing.* Tracing the following straight and curved lines is a sophisticated hand and eye coordination test.

SPACE AND FORM PERCEPTION

A. Space perception activities—position in space, gross spatial relation, and finer spatial relations

a) *Rope Obstacle Course.* Tie fifteen to twenty ropes horizontally across a hallway or narrow room. The height above the floor should range from six inches to two to three feet. They should be spaced about two feet apart. Have the children step over the low ropes and climb over the high ones, seeing how close they can come without actually touching them.

Variations include reducing the intervals at which the ropes
are spaced and increasing the number of ropes. Then, have
the child alternate going over and under the ropes, no matter
what height they are. Let the children compete against
each other for time. .

b) *Playground.* All playground equipment requires relating the
whole body to a greater space. This equipment helps the
spatial attributes of height.

c) *Pacing off Distances.* Many situations can be used to learn
some kind of spatial concept. If the children are going for
a walk, stop them a few feet from an upright object such
as a tree or telephone pole. Place one child about four feet
from the tree and another about six feet from it. Ask the
other children which child is closest to the tree. Have them
check their answers by pacing off the two distances or use
a rope to measure the distances. A more difficult task is
asking the children guess how many footsteps there are
between each child and the tree.

d) *Go In and Out the Window.* To help the children visualize
their own height and width, divide them into two groups. The
first join hands and forms a circle. The second stands behind
those in the circle. The group with their hands joined have
varying distances between their bodies and hold their hands
at varying heights. The children in the second group move
in and out of the hands in the circle, seeing how close they
can come to the arms above and the legs alongside without
actually touching them. They may enjoy singing the following
song as they go:

> *Go in and out the window,*
> *Go in and out the window,*
> *Go in and out the window,*
> *As we have done before.*

e) *Swiss Cheese Box.* A large cardboard box with various holes
cut out of it will allow the child to experiment with his
body dimensions. He will gain experience in what he will and
will not fit through.

f) *Rope Stretch.* Ropes can be used in spatial training. Lay down
an eight-foot jump rope at the end of the auditorium wall next
to the child. Ask the child to tell you how many lengths of
rope laid end to end will it take to go the length of the room.

g) *Ladder Games.* One of the most useful pieces of equipment to gain experience moving through exact space is the ladder. Two helpful games are:

(1) Lay the ladder at right angles to the floor. The child moves in and out of the rungs, crawling, spider walking, etc.

(2) While the ladder is supported on either end by chairs, the child goes under two rungs, up through the next, steps into the next five, and so on.

h) *Hoop Hop.* Half of the class holds hoops in front of them. Some hold them on the floor, others a few inches off the floor. The children form a zig-zag line by having every other child take one step backwards. The other half of the class move in various ways such as crawl, walk backwards, bear walk, etc., through, around and under the hoops. Have the children trade places after the first group is finished.

i) *Route Tracing.* Very simple map following is accomplished by laying a network of different colored lines on the playground. Each line may be followed through to the end. Give the child a "map" that illustrates a route through the network, using various "roads". The map should be colored to help him find the correct line. A sample course might have the child start on green, turn left on red, follow red until it crosses yellow, then follow that until it hits green again.

j) *Rope Maze.* To teach moving through exact space, fifteen to twenty short rope segments can be put down in various patterns (see diagrams) to form mazes. The children elephant walk, crawl, etc., through the maze. Ask the children if they can see their path through to where they started.

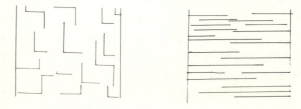

k) *Box Trail.* To teach following a spatial map, lay down a series of boxes on the grass in an organized pattern. The child is given a cardboard map depicting the pattern, and a trail is marked for him to follow. When he reaches the destination, the last box can contain a reward, such as his name on a piece of paper, a new set of instructions, a tidbit to eat, etc.

B. Form perception activities—recognition of forms other than printed letters and words (shape, size, color, brightness)

a) *Sorting.* Using various sizes of colored and shaped geometric forms, have the child sort according to various criteria. Some of these might be: sort to size regardless of color, sort to color regardless of size, sort to shape regardless of the other features, and so on.

b) *Pattern Recognition.* A good way to strengthen a child's ability to observe likenesses of shape is to have him match pictures of objects in color and perspective to outlines of those same objects drawn in trace outline only. Cut colorful photos of various readily identifiable objects from magazines and paste them to cards. Trace with black crayon a simple outline of the central object of each picture onto white paper. Space the colored pictures at regular intervals along a chalk ledge and have the child put the outline diagram next to the picture it matches.

c) *Block Shapes.* Using blocks which vary only slightly in size and shape (same color, if possible), present the child with a single block on one table. On the next table, present numerous blocks, including one which is identical to that on the first table. Can the child, without placing the blocks side by side, identify the two blocks that match?

d) *Form Identification.* Show the children a geometric form such as a circle or rectangle and ask them to identify all similarly shaped objects in the room, such as clocks, wheels, hoops, tabletops, crayon boxes, books, etc.

e) *Building Blocks.* With blocks of wood or corrugated cardboard, have the children build a structure that looks like something in a picture (for example, a cabinet, telephone pole, house, etc.).

f) *Matching Blocks.* Give each child a block of any shape, as long as it has a matching block. Scatter the other blocks of various sizes and shapes on the floor, between four and eight feet away. Have each child identify the block that is the mate of the one he holds.

g) *Beads.* Have the child find a square bead in a box of rounds beads, all of which are the same color.

h) *Bead Sorting.* Have the children sort beads according to color, shape and size.

i) *Old Maid.* The card game "Old Maid" offers the opportunity to match forms.

j) *Shape Recognition.* Viewing different shapes, such as a square, triangle, cube, tetrahedron, etc., from different angles can be used to teach recognition. Have the children try to identify the shape correctly even if placed at an unusual angle.

k) *Form Perception Tag.* A group of children are lined up on one side of the room. Each child has a piece of cardboard which has been cut into a geometric shape. The object of the game is to run across the room eluding the person who is "it". The tagged children then join the child who is "it", trying to catch the the rest of the group. The children trade off their cardboard shapes after each run.

C. Figure ground activities

(*Note:* See the section on Postural and Bilateral Integration for reflex inhibition activities to precede this section, as well as the activities listed under Activities for Tactile Defensiveness.)

a) *I See Something.* One student looks around and picks out an object somewhere in the room. The remainder of the students try to figure out what the object is. Questions are asked until the object is identified. The game can be made more challenging by choosing objects in pictures or puzzles.

b) *Walk the Colored Line.* Draw several criss-crossing lines on the sidewalk with chalk, or lay down several differently colored pieces of rope. Vary the color and size, as well as the amount of overlap. Have the child follow the path of only one color, disregarding the others.

c) *Hoop Maze.* Lay fifteen or twenty hoops on the ground so they overlap each other. Place among them four or five hoops of a different color. Have the children run or jump through this maze, placing their feet only in the hoops of a different color.

d) *Simple Jigsaw Puzzles.* Ask the child to reassemble puzzles made from simple cut up magazine pictures. First, separate the foreground from the background in a few parts. Next, cut out specific objects. Later, see how many elements can be separated with the child still being able to reassemble them.

e) *Scribble Trail.* Have the child scribble on a large piece of paper with several different colored pens. Then see if he can follow the "trail" of one specific color without losing his line.

f) *Activities with Printed Materials.* Use a series of magazine pictures or textbook illustrations to have the child pick out as many of the small details as possible. Progress to using a printed page on which the child is asked to pick out all of a particular word or letter combination. For example, have the child mark all the words that begin with, "bo" or mark all the "the" words that appear.

g) *Newspaper Reading.* Ask the child to identify certain numbers, letters, words and titles in the classified section of a newspaper.

h) *Commercial Products.* A number of commercially available products have useful figure/ground worksheets in them.

TACTILE DEFENSIVENESS

a) *Beanbag Obstacle Course.* Holding a beanbag or similar object in one hand, the child assumes a quadrupedal position. Keeping the hand holding the beanbag off the floor, have him proceed through an obstacle course.

b) *Coffee Grinder.* Have the child place one hand on the floor, with his arm extended and the other shoulder pointed straight up. Keeping the body erect, he "walks" his feet around the pivoting point of the arm. Have him change arms and directions frequently.

c) *Scooter Spin.* Lying prone on a scooter board, the child rests on one hand and spins himself with the other, keeping the scooter over a mark on the floor.

d) *Incline Board Activities.* Coming off an inclined ramp on a scooter, the child can do one of several unilateral activities:

(1) Place one hand on the floor and start and maintain a slow spinning motion as forward momentum continues.

(2) Use the instructor's hand as a pivot point.

(3) Go around a box, using one hand as a pivot guide.

(4) Pick up bowling pins and move them to another place.

(5) Grab a suspended inner tube strip with one hand while maintaining motion.

e) *Maypole Paddle.* Two children lie prone on scooters, which are attached to a pole by a rope. As they "paddle" around the pole, the second child tries to catch the first before they are "wound up." One or the other hand can be used for propulsion, but to enhance disorders of the left side, the left hand is preferred.